That Was the...

Best Party Ever!

How to Give Birthday Parties Kids Will <u>Never</u> Forget

by Sharron Werlin Krull
with Mary Humphrey
illustrated by Ann Humphrey Williams

EDITOR: Mary Humphrey
COVER & ILLUSTRATIONS: Ann Humphrey Williams
PHOTOGRAPHY: Timothy Burman
PRINTER: Gall House Printing

ISBN 1-885650-03-5 (pbk.)
Library of Congress Catalog Card Number: 95-092669

1ST PRINTING 1995

Published by:
PLAY POWER
1365 St. Catherine Court
Concord, Ca. 94521
(510) 680-4390

Manufactured in the United States of America

Here's what people are saying about Sharron Werlin Krull...

"Sharron Werlin Krull is the Charlotte Mailliard of the toddler-to-ten set. She throws parties for kids -- and she doesn't fool around when it comes to having fun."

- San Francisco Examiner

"She arrives armed with art supplies that turn ordinary lunch bags into goody sacks, a treasure chest filled with trinkets for prizes and a schedule that keeps the kids hopping every minute for two hours."

- Diablo Magazine

"Everybody wins, nobody loses with real party animal. "We never play games where one child wins and another loses. There's no place for tears at a birthday party.""

- The Tribune

"A successful party doesn't just happen. The most important thing to remember is that kids just want to play and have a good time."

- Woman Magazine

About the Author ~ Sharron Werlin Krull

"That Was the Best Party Ever!" is the latest publication from this high energy and dynamic early childhood expert. When she's not directing and teaching at a local cooperative pre-school, instructing college students or giving keynote speeches and workshops, Sharron spends her time creating and giving great children's parties. Over the years, thousands of kids have enjoyed her parties including the children of sports stars Joe Montana and Dwight Clark.

Sharron is the co-author of two teacher resource books, "Circle Time Activities for Young Children" and "Play Power Games and Activities for Young Children." She's also produced two instructional videos. Her party-giving talents have been featured in several national magazines and major newspapers. The San Francisco Examiner calls her "the Pied Piper of Parties." Sharron lives in Concord, California with her husband Steve. They enjoy the beach, sun, surf and each other, not necessarily in that order!

About the Illustrator ~ Ann Humphrey Williams

Ann can't remember a time when she hasn't loved having a pencil, pen or paintbrush in her hand. Her first work of art was a mural drawn on the bathroom floor with lipstick when she was three. Her mother says the drawing made her laugh so hard she hated to scrub it off.

Ann received a Fine Arts degree from U.C. Davis then moved to British Columbia where she lived on the edge of a rain forest, earned her teaching credential, illustrated educational and marketing material and taught elementary school for 10 years.

She now lives in Lafayette, California with her husband, Maurice, sons, Tim, Benjamin and Braden, Ernie the dog, two cats, three chickens, a parakeet, a spotted gecko, two goldfish and a praying mantis, all of whom show up in her illustrations from time to time and provide inspiration and insight into life's humorous and whimsical aspects.

About the Editor ~ Mary Humphrey

Mary is a recent escapee from the corporate world where she wrote business cases, strategic plans, RFP's and mission statements. "I was living the part of a Dilbert comic strip character," she says. When the company offered a golden handshake (well, maybe more of a tin handshake) she decided to take them up on it and see how real people live.

Mary now works as a freelance writer and editor. She develops marketing material for businesses and writes technical articles, documentation, children's books and how-to books. The *other* 40 hours of the week, Mary co-owns and operates the Leapfrog Contractor Referral company in Walnut Creek, California. "It's hard work, but I love it," she says. "I'd never go back and would recommend the step I took to anyone --- who loves adventure and has nerves of steel!"

Dedicated to...

all the children who, years later, still say,
"Thanks, Sharron. Y'know, I still remember my party.
That was the best party ever!"

and to my husband, Steve, for his support, love and
encouragement. I couldn't have done it without him.

and special thanks to...

Tomi Matthews

Sue O'Malley

Meg Freedman

Kelly Kutchera

who helped me in ways both big and small

TABLE OF CONTENTS

Why Kids Love These Parties!

Ages & Stages

Get Ready! Get Set! Let's Party!!

Theme Parties Kids Love

Catalog Shopping Sources

Indexes

The Party Animal Says:

For a fun and *safe* party, provide adult supervision for all party activities!

STOP!

This is no ordinary birthday party book. Why is it different? This book is written from a different perspective...the point of view of a child development specialist with her primary focus on the children and how they grow and learn: socially, emotionally, cognitively and physically.

Kids have different needs at different ages and stages. The games and activities in this book are designed to be age appropriate. The ideas and suggestions come from years of teaching, observing and listening to kids.

The kids are the ones who inspire me and keep me thinking and coming up with new ideas. I hope this book conveys my experience, energy and enthusiasm for giving birthday parties kids will never forget!

Please...

take the time to read the introductory sections so you can understand the many different ways you can make your child's birthday party memorable. Then refer to the Table of Contents to find *the* party your child wants. Years later, you'll still hear,

"That was the best party ever!"

A KID-TESTED PARTY PHILOSOPHY

I've conducted hundreds of parties for children of all ages. The parties in this book are the ones kids tell me they love the most. They're the *best parties ever!* Kids take such delight in the hoopla and fanfare surrounding their birthdays, I suggest you celebrate three ways:

✳ a family party　　✳ a party with friends　　✳ a school party

In the Spotlight!

Here's the key to making memories your child will treasure forever:

On just this one special day, out of all the days in the year, let your birthday hot shot take the spotlight. On just this one day, let your child have *all* the power, make *all* the decisions and be *first* in every activity!

Make it a Special Day

I promise, taking the spotlight for an hour and a half or two out of all the hours in the year will *not* spoil your child! Your child's peers will not only *accept* the idea of the birthday child taking the spotlight, they will *expect* it because it's exactly what they want at their parties. They expect to:

- be the leader,
- be first at the games,
- lick the frosting off the candles,
- eat the first bite of cake, and
- keep the decorations from the top of the cake.

Of course, I don't mean your birthday child shouldn't be polite, cooperative and considerate. Good manners can go hand-in-hand with being the star. Here's an example Emily Post would agree with: When you serve the cake, serve all the other children first, but ask them to wait for the birthday child to take the first bite. That will be their signal to begin eating.

The Case Against Competitive Games

Have you ever watched children play Pin the Tail on the Donkey? Everyone laughs at the uncoordinated kids with no sense of direction who miss the target by a mile. Those kids might be "good sports" on the outside and join in the laughter, but inside they may feel embarrassed and humiliated.

Or how about Musical Chairs? When the music stops, the kids push and shove to get a chair. The first loser sits out all alone. As the game continues, the kids get more and more aggressive. They stop at nothing to be the winner. In the meantime, the losers feel left out...some of them are in tears.

These games are prime examples of competitive games and the reason I recommend only cooperative games, where every child's a winner. Competitive games pit children against each other. They teach children that, if you shove, push, hit or trip, you might beat the other players and win. There's just one winner and a whole bunch of losers. Children play games to have fun and be involved. They don't want to be eliminated, rejected, left out or hurt physically or emotionally. (Who does?!!)

Every Child's a Winner!

Cooperative games include everyone. Every child is "in." There's no pressure to win, no fear or anxiety about losing. Cooperative games make kids feel good about themselves and others. They promote self-esteem, sharing, kindness and teamwork.

Every game and activity in this book is stimulating, challenging and geared for success.

What if Suzy Doesn't Want to Play?

Don't force guests to play games if they don't want to. Allow children to watch and join in when they're ready. On the other hand, don't offer alternatives (e.g., to play in your child's bedroom) as this may encourage other guests to choose to leave the game. Offer two choices: join the game or watch the game. You might even say, "We always need an audience!"

Include Your Child From Start To Finish

Beginning at age four, most children receive a great deal of joy and satisfaction from helping plan their parties. Talk to your birthday child about his or her expectations. You may be surprised to find they're quite different from yours. Spend time together to go over each area that needs to be planned and organized. Pick a theme and decide on the games and activities. Include your child in all the shopping, too.

My philosophy is simple: birthday parties are for kids (and, of course, the kid in us, no matter what our age!) -- involve them, make them feel special. It's their day. I can't think of a better gift, or a better self-esteem booster, than to say "I love you" by celebrating the day your child was born.

A great party doesn't just happen. It takes both planning and organization. But, it really isn't that difficult and you *can* do it! I'll provide you with proven tips on all aspects of giving parties, from the invitations to saying goodbye to the guests. I'll share surefire strategies for avoiding typical party pitfalls and give you suggestions for refreshments, prizes and kid-tested formats and themes.

> *PARTY ANIMAL REMINDER:*
>
> *Keep*
> *It*
> *Smart 'n*
> *Simple!*

But, while there's a wealth of information in this book, your imagination and ingenuity will be your greatest asset. Feel free to adapt the ideas you find here, don't panic and, above all, have fun. You'll throw a great party and the kids will love it.

THE FAMILY PARTY:

TIME FOR TRADITIONS

If you can, hold the family party on your child's actual birthday. Make the whole day a celebration!

- Wake the birthday child up by singing a "Happy Birthday" song.

- Serve a special treat for breakfast -- how about teddy bear pancakes?

- Give your special girl or boy a gift in the morning.

- Make a badge or pin for your child to wear that announces "Today I'm _____ years old."

This is the time to establish family traditions and rituals.

If this is your child's first birthday, buy a twelve year candle and light it each year.

Pizza and Jell-O?

Plan a special birthday dinner and cake. Let the birthday child decide the menu, even if it's pizza and Jell-O! (As your child grows, so will his or her tastes. Before you know it, the menu will be steak and lobster!) Serve the cake on a special birthday plate.

Extend the Family

Include older siblings in planning the family birthday celebration and the party with friends, too. They'll love doing it and their help will be a great boon for you.

Invite siblings, grandparents, aunts, uncles, cousins and all the rest of the relatives living nearby. Don't forget to include other significant adults in your child's life: babysitters, nannies, godparents, etc.

THE SCHOOL PARTY

Ask the Teacher

Pre-school, kindergarten and primary grade teachers usually do something to recognize the birthday child. Teachers often have a birthday ritual which is conducted exactly the same way for each child in the class. For instance, they may let the birthday child wear a special hat, crown or badge and be the leader for the day.

Many schools send out information at the beginning of the year about how and when children's birthdays will be celebrated. If you did not receive this sort of information (or if now, when you need it, you can't find it!) give your child's teacher a call.

Donate a Book...It Beats Cupcakes!

Find out from the teacher if there are specific things he or she would like you to provide. For example, the teacher may ask for:

- photos or biographical data to read, share or put on a bulletin board.

- cookies or a non-sugary treat. Plain sugar cookies shaped like numbers are a great choice. (Teachers and maintenance personnel don't usually appreciate crumbly cupcakes.)

- small party favors.

- Or, instead of treats, the teacher may ask if you'd like to donate a book, tape, puzzle or small piece of classroom equipment in honor of your child's birthday. (If the teacher doesn't suggest it, you might want to. What a great way to help our schools and save on dental bills!)

If your child takes treats or party favors, remember to include enough for every child in the class. Don't forget the teacher and teacher's aides, too.

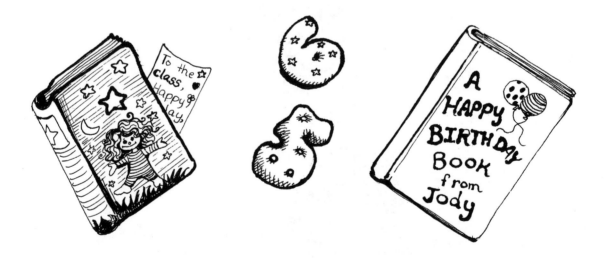

TIP:
If your child's birthday falls on a holiday or during vacation months, ask the teacher if there's a special day for celebrating those birthdays or if you may pick a day to celebrate the birthday or half-birthday.

THE PARTY
WITH FRIENDS

The party with friends is the most important celebration for your birthday child. This party is the primary focus of this book.

The Preview

Here's what you'll find in the pages that follow:

1. Ideas for tailoring the party to your child's age and stage.

2. Advice for parties for twins and other multiples.

3. Tips from a party pro about the "what, where, when and who" of successful birthday parties.

4. Lots of good ideas for decorations, refreshments, party bags and favors, serving the cake, and winding down after the party.

The Real Thing!

Finally, you'll find the theme parties. That's where the fun *really* begins!

The THEME PARTIES KIDS LOVE section gives you detailed instructions for great parties for children age four and up. But, please, don't skip all the good stuff in between. After you read it, you'll be able to fine tune any party to fit your child's unique personality and developmental level.

AGES & STAGES

Each child is a wonderfully special and unique individual. When you plan a birthday party consider and respect your child's personality and temperament. The party you think of as fun and exciting might feel overwhelming and too stimulating to your child. Tune the party to your child's age and stage and you and your birthday child will have fun.

Take two year olds, for instance. Some two year olds are sweet and cooperative at their birthday parties; Others fit the description of typically tyrannical two's in "Terrific Two's" to a tee.

Most children display a mixture of patterns, sometimes reaching a stage three months early, sometimes skipping it, other times reaching it six months later than you expected. Once in a while, your child will surprise you by reverting to patterns you thought were long gone.

The ideas you'll find in the following pages fit the "typical" stages according to child development studies. I hope you'll find them helpful in planning a wonderful and memorable birthday party just right for your child's age and stage.

WONDERFUL ONE'S

I absolutely refuse to conduct parties for one year olds! The one year old does not understand the concept of a birthday. What the parents really hire me for is to keep the small fry together in one place and entertained while the parents socialize.

That may be nice for the adults, but it completely misses the point of a birthday party. Don't waste your money on a party professional or entertainer for your one year old. Save it for an older child's birthday party (four and up) when the child can help plan the party.

Now, I'm not saying you shouldn't celebrate your child's first birthday. Not a chance. A child's first birthday is a very special occasion. It's a landmark that should be celebrated. But recognize this celebration for what it is -- a party for the proud parents of the birthday child!

A Party You <u>and</u> Your One Year Old Will Enjoy

Here's an idea for a party you *and* your one year old will enjoy: Hold an open house during the birthday child's best time of day. Serve food buffet style. Finger foods, small sandwiches, not-too-messy salads, cake, ice cream and beverages work well.

*   Ask parents of small children to keep an eye on their own little ones.

*   *Don't* plan any formal games or activities

*   *Do* go through the ritual of putting a candle on the cake and singing "Happy Birthday." Help your birthday child blow out the candle.

Start Some Traditions

This is a time to start traditions. Make sure you and your spouse discuss and agree on the traditions you want to establish for your children. Think back on your own birthdays. Here are some ideas:

- Choose a special birthday song to sing.

- Buy a twelve-year candle and light it on each of your child's first twelve birthdays.

- Start the tradition of putting an extra candle on the cake for "one to grow on" or "one for good luck."

Take lots of pictures and videos. These will be the only way your child will be able to recall his or her first birthday. Of course, *you* will always remember it!

TERRIFIC

TWO'S

Two year olds do not take turns, play fair or act nice to visitors! Usually they barely understand the concept of a party. Do not expect them to share, play cooperatively or be polite. Quite the contrary! Typical two's are grabby, pushy, demanding, possessive and socially immature. The Toddler Property Laws shown below pretty much sum up this age and stage:

TODDLER PROPERTY LAWS

- If I like it, it's mine.

- If it's in my hand, it's mine.

- If I can take it from you, it's mine.

- If I had it a little while ago, it's mine.

- If it's mine, it must *never* appear to be yours in *any* way.

- If I'm doing or building something, all the pieces are mine.

- If it looks just like mine, it *is* mine.

Tune Into Your Two Year Old

Obviously, reason and logic are not part of a two year old's way of thinking! You may be wondering by now why on earth you'd want to attempt a birthday party for a child this age! Two year olds do enjoy the company of other children even though they cannot share easily.

You can have a successful party for your two year old if you keep your expectations in line with your two year old's temperament and abilities. Two year olds...

- ❀ Play side-by-side (parallel play) rather than with other children (cooperative play),

- ❀ Have very short attention spans, and

- ❀ Are constantly on the move.

ADVICE FROM A REAL PARTY ANIMAL:

Your two year olds' expectations will definitely be influenced by experience with other birthday parties, e.g., for older siblings. In general, simpler is better. After all, how many of us even remember our second birthdays?

Party Ideas

- Specify in the invitations that one parent must attend with each toddler guest.

- Schedule the party for a time that does not interfere with toddler nap-times.

- Plan for the party to last about 1 to 1-1/2 hours.

- If you can get away with it, include just the immediate family and a nearby relative or two.

- Serve a cake or cupcakes with candles but *skip the ice cream* --- it isn't worth the bother or the mess!

- Your two year old will be delighted with presents, especially by tearing off the wrapping!

If you and your child are part of a playgroup (parents and toddlers who meet on a regular basis so the children can learn to play together and parents get a chance to socialize), plan your two year old's party on a day when you host the playgroup at your house or at a local park or playground.

Keep It Loose

Don't plan any structured games - keep it loose and informal. If you have the party indoors, set up designated party areas. Provide a variety of toys (favorites include Duplos, large colored building blocks, stacking toys, take-apart toys, simple puzzles, etc.) and set up some special interest stations. These could include Playdough, a sandbox and water play.

Invisible Painting

Give the toddler guests small plastic buckets and shovels to play with in the sand. You can even fill the buckets with water and give each child a small, inexpensive paintbrush from the hardware store. The children can paint the sidewalk, trees or any other surface easily, joyfully and with no lasting effect!

> *TIP:*
>
> *The plastic buckets, shovels & paint brushes make terrific take-home favors!*

Bubble Chase

Get the parents involved by giving each one a bottle of store-bought bubbles. They can blow bubbles for the toddlers to chase, catch and pop. It's a great way to expend all that toddler energy and spend quality time together.

Water Fun

Two year olds love water play. Fill a plastic tub or basin with water (kitty litter pans from the supermarket are the perfect size). Provide dolls and water toys such as plastic containers, pitchers, measuring cups, small sponges, scoops, funnels, strainers, rubber animals, boats, trucks, etc. Poke holes in some of the containers so the kids can make it rain.

And Playdough, Of Course!

Set up a Playdough Station by spreading a plastic tablecloth on the floor. Provide cookie cutters, small rolling pins, plastic knives and garlic presses. Of course, the toddlers' own fingers will be their favorite tools for molding, pounding, squeezing and manipulating.

Here's my favorite Playdough recipe. I've found it to be far superior to any sold commercially. Just store it in an airtight plastic bag - it needs no refrigeration - and it will last for months. Make an extra batch and divide it into smaller plastic bags to send home with each guest as a party favor.

PLAYDOUGH RECIPE

Ingredients

2 cups flour
1 cup salt
4 teaspoons cream of tartar
2 cups water
3 tablespoons oil
food coloring or Liquid Watercolor

Instructions

1. Add food coloring or Liquid Watercolor to water.

2. Combine all ingredients and mix together in sauce pan.

3. Cook over medium heat. Stir constantly until the dough thickens, pulls away from the sides of the pan and gathers into a big ball.

4. Place the dough on the countertop and let it cool until just warm.

5. Knead the dough for 3-4 minutes.

6. Store in a plastic bag until ready to use.

Try Some Tunes!

Here are some songs toddlers enjoy. Gather everyone into a circle, and prepare for fun and laughter!

Ring Around The Rosie

Ring around the rosie.
A pocket full of posies.
Ashes, ashes we all fall down!

❀ Gather children into a circle and show them how to walk around the circle holding hands and chanting the rhyme.

❀ Everyone falls down on the ground at the end of the rhyme.

❀ Now, while you're all on the ground, lead children in singing the next verse.

The cows are in the meadow,
They're eating buttercups.
Flowers, flowers, we all stand up!

❀ Everyone stands up at the end of the verse and once again holds hands, walking around in a circle as they repeat the first verse..."Ring around the rosie..."

❀ Give children plenty of time to repeat this singing game over and over. It's a favorite!

Itsy Bitsy Spider

The itsy-bitsy spider
Went up the water spout.

✳ Use the first and middle fingers of one hand to walk up the inside of your opposite forearm.

Down came the rain and

✳ Stretch your arms up over your head, then bring them slowly down, waving your hands from side to side and wiggling your fingers.

Washed the spider out.

✳ Bring your arms together in front of you, crossing your hands, then quickly swing them down and out.

**Out came the sun and
Dried up all the rain.**

❋ Make a circle with your arms
above your head.

**And the itsy-bitsy spider
Went up the spout again.**

❋ Use your fingers to walk up your
opposite forearm again.

"Itsy Bitsy Spider" is not only a rainy day song but a sing-it-again-everyday song.
You can vary it to the children's delight. Try singing "The Huge, Enormous
Spider" in a loud, deep voice or "The Very Quiet Spider" in a whisper.

Uh Oh! *The Party Animal sees kids sitting with their legs
"W" style. Kids often like to sit this way but encourage
them not to. It can harm their hips and knees, eventually
leading to arthritis and other physical problems. Instead,
tell the kids to sit "Criss-Cross Applesauce" with their
knees out and ankles crossed. It's much healthier!*

FUN THREE'S

Meet Mr. and Ms. Congeniality

The three year old is a rather happy person -- friendly, agreeable and sociable -- who enjoys a party. Your three year old may not totally understand what a party is; only that it's for her or him. At this age, your child knows a party is special and she or he's excited about getting to play with friends.

Free Play's the Ticket

Don't try to play any structured games. Three year olds enjoy free play more. Settings three year olds enjoy include:

🐇**parks,**

🐇**playgrounds,**

🐇**children's gyms,**

🐇**pre-schools, and**

🐇**their own backyards or playrooms.**

Three year olds vary in their abilities to handle social situations. Some will need a parent to stay the entire time (the extreme introvert or the out-of-bounds extrovert), others will behave better without a parent present. In fact, your own child may not be able to handle being in the limelight.

Party Hits

The three year old's party should be no longer than 1-1/2 hours. Plan activities that alternate between active (a hunt or parade) and quiet (making necklaces or opening presents). This will help you keep their attention and *your* sanity!

You can adapt many of the ideas in the THEME PARTIES KIDS LOVE section for your three year old's party or try these sure-to-please favorites.

Hidden Treasure

A treasure hunt is a winner for any age group and especially for three year olds. Match the hunt to the party's theme. Girls and boys this age both like toy rings and bracelets. Hide enough so each guest can find one ring and one bracelet for each hand. (Let kids know the "legal" limit ahead of time.)

Parade

Kids love to march in parades. Provide each guest with a store-bought or homemade musical instrument. They can easily make some fun instruments themselves following the instructions below. I suggest you provide only one kind of instrument. Otherwise a child may decide he or she wants the one Johnny has. With three year olds' short attention spans, I can almost guarantee this will happen.

Toilet Paper Tube Kazoo

Materials:

cardboard toilet paper tube
water-based markers
stickers
wax paper
rubber bands
pencil or hole punch

Directions:

1. Decorate the tube with markers and stickers.

2. Punch a hole about 2" from one end of the tube with a hole punch or pencil.

3. Cut out a circle of wax paper. Use it to cover the other end of the tube and secure it with a rubber band.

4. Blow or hum into the open end to make great sounds.

Ta Dahhhh!

1.

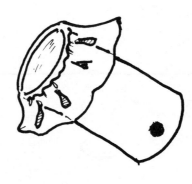

2.

3.

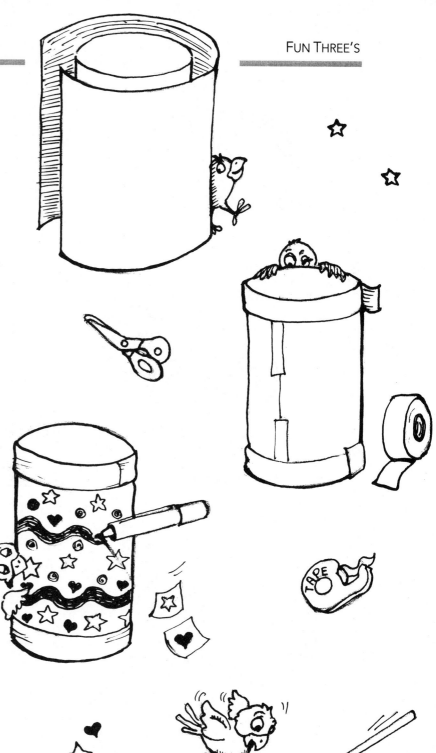

Oatmeal Box Drum

Materials:

oatmeal box, salt carton or
coffee can
water-based markers
stickers
construction paper or paper
grocery bag
tape or glue
scissors
disposable chopsticks

Directions:

1. Cut construction paper
   or grocery bag to wrap
   around the outside of
   the cylinder.

2. Wrap paper around the
   container and secure
   with tape or glue.

3. Decorate with markers
   and stickers.

4. You're now ready to tap
   a great tune with your
   chopstick drumsticks!

Paper Plate Tambourine

Materials:

paper plates
stapler
stickers
water based markers
popcorn kernels, dry beans,
peas, rice or pebbles

Directions:

1. Fold the paper plate in half.

2. Drop in some popcorn kernels, pebbles, etc.

3. Staple the plate together, all around the edges.

4. Decorate with markers and stickers.

5. Shake, rattle and roll!

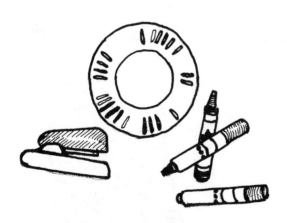

Merry Melodies

"Baa, Baa" and the two songs which follow it can all be sung to the same tune. If you can't remember this childhood classic, just ask a kid (big or little!)

BAA, BAA BLACK SHEEP

Baa, baa black sheep have you any wool?
Yes sir, yes sir, three bags full.
One for my master and one for my dame.
One for the little boy who lives down the lane.
Baa, baa black sheep have you any wool?
Yes sir, yes sir, three bags full.

Twinkle, Twinkle Little Star

Twinkle, twinkle little star
✧ hold both hands up, open and
close fingers like twinkling stars

How I wonder what you are
✧ touch both sides of your head
with your index fingers

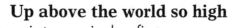

Up above the world so high
✧ point your index fingers up
toward the sky

Like a diamond in the sky
✧ form a diamond shape by placing your thumbs together and index fingers together

Twinkle, twinkle little star
✧ hold hands up again, open and close your fingers

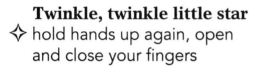

How I wonder what you are
✧ touch both sides of your head again with your index fingers

Notice the kids sitting correctly with legs "Criss-Cross Applesauce!"

THE ALPHABET SONG

A B C D, E F G
H I J K L M N O P
Q R S T U V
W X Y and Z.
Now I've sung my ABC's
Next time won't you sing with me?

Here's a favorite tot tune with a different "twist."

I'M A LITTLE TEAPOT

**I'm a little teapot, short and stout.
Here is my handle,**

Put one hand on hip

Here is my spout.

Bend other arm, elbow at waist,
forearm pointing out to the side

**When I get all steamed up,
then I shout,
"Just tip me over and pour me out!"**

Bend at the waist as if pouring
from your "spout"

**I'm a very clever pot, its true.
Here's an example
of what I can do.
I can change my handle and
change my spout.**

Change position of hands, so
spout is on the opposite side.

Just tip me over and pour me out.

Bend body in opposite direction

Edible Necklace

Tie a piece of wagon wheel pasta onto one end of a piece of elastic cord or twine to keep the goodies from sliding off. Let the kids string the cord with Froot Loops, Cheerios, miniature twist pretzels, etc. When they're done, tie the ends together for a beautiful and tasty necklace.

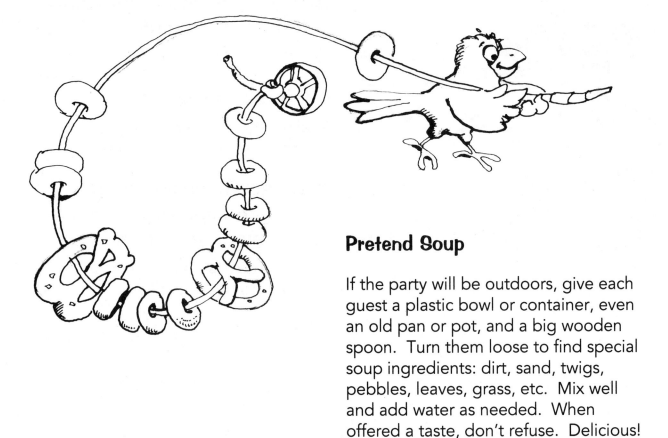

Pretend Soup

If the party will be outdoors, give each guest a plastic bowl or container, even an old pan or pot, and a big wooden spoon. Turn them loose to find special soup ingredients: dirt, sand, twigs, pebbles, leaves, grass, etc. Mix well and add water as needed. When offered a taste, don't refuse. Delicious!

Party Bags

Buy white, lunch-size paper bags for the guests to use to make party bags. Supply an assortment of markers (water-based markers are best), stickers, stamps and stamp pads for the guests to create and decorate their very own party bags. Be sure to write names on the bags to prevent confusion.

FANTASTIC FOUR'S

These Kids Know How to Party!

Four year olds know what a party is and how to party! You'll need at least one adult for every three or four children and plenty of planned activities.

Four year olds love action and are creatures of boundless energy and enthusiasm. Limit the parties to 1-1/2 to 2 hours. Any longer and they'll wear themselves (and you) out.

Plan short games. Four year olds have a hard time waiting for their turns. And keep the games simple. Children this age are not mature enough to understand or appreciate complex games.

Four's Can Be Fickle

Don't be alarmed if your four year old announces to his or her best friend, "You're not my friend and you're not invited to my birthday party." Four's can be fickle. This is typical of the age. I suggest you disregard your four year old's whimsical changes of mind. He or she will likely change it back again the next day or minute when things are once again going his or her way.

Stickers and Other Fun Stuff

Usually four year olds love stickers. A favorite activity is for each guest to create a party bag by covering the whole thing with stickers.

Most four year olds will easily accept the games you suggest, the food you serve and the party favors you buy. Everybody, including you and your four year old, will have a great time at the party!

Four is the perfect age for a theme party. Take a look at the parties for this age group in the THEME PARTIES KIDS LOVE section for some memory-making super-hit party ideas.

FRIENDLY FIVE'S

This is the big one!

The five year old birthday is the *big* one for most kids. They wait for it, counting every day, anticipate it excitedly, plan it meticulously. Your five year old will probably be very clear about what kind of party he or she wants. Listen carefully and accommodate your birthday child's wishes and desires even though they may not be what you had envisioned.

Listen to Your Birthday Child

I heard one well-meaning parent relate the story of her son's party. He really wanted to have a theme based on the latest superhero on the market. Mom thought a firefighter theme would be nice. So he had a firefighter party...much to his chagrin and disappointment.

Your child will be five only once. This birthday is very important to every five year old. Let your birthday child help with planning and shopping. Pick out the party favors together. Follow your child's suggestions about who to invite (try to talk him or her out of inviting the whole class!)

Theme parties work well for this age. Check the THEME PARTIES KIDS LOVE section for ideas. Once again, 1-1/2 to 2 hours is an ideal length of time for a five year old's party. If anything, you should *overplan*. Have games and activities ready for every minute of the party and every minute will be fun for you and your birthday child.

HIGH ENERGY SIXES THROUGH TWELVE'S

Energy Personified

Six to twelve year olds have one major characteristic in common: Energy! Plan parties accordingly, with lots of action. I mean, plan every minute! Even overplan!! Theme parties work well for kids this age, particularly for the six to nine year olds.

Between the ages of eight and ten (it varies for each child), your child will likely go through an "I hate boys" or "I hate girls" stage. It's perfectly OK to host an all-boy or all-girl event.

No Party Poopers!

I've heard so many kids this age tell me how disappointed they were when their parents ignored their party requests. Happy or sad, the memories will last a lifetime. Make your child's birthday memories happy ones. Abide by your child's wishes and make birthday planning serious business! We do this for adults turning 40, why not for kids turning ____? (Fill in the blank.)

Once kids enter school, they love social situations such as parties with friends. They relish the idea of parties with all the trimmings, enjoy traditions and look forward to their birthday parties with eager anticipation.

At this age, kids see birthday parties as statements of who they are. Don't downplay the significance of your child's birthday celebration. This is not the time to make a birthday "no big deal" because it *is* a big deal to your birthday child.

Presents, We Like Presents!

Kids know that the more *guests* at their parties, the more *presents* they'll receive. Six to nine year olds, in particular, tend to want to invite *lots* of guests (and therefore receive *lots* of gifts!).

Be patient...as your child matures, he or she will probably be happy to invite just a friend or two to spend the day at an amusement park or sleep overnight.

Two Hours Max

A two hour party is plenty long for this age group just as for the other age groups. If you take the kids to an amusement park, though, you might as well plan on all day. I haven't come across any parks yet that sell two-hour passes. Save money by taking a picnic lunch to all-day events.

Aww, Gross! That's For Babies.

As they get older, many kids would rather skip the party favors and decorations and substitute amusement park games and rides. Often, they prefer to forgo blowing out candles on a cake. You can reserve this for the family birthday party.

If you're conducting the birthday party, don't mention the word "games." Instead, start right in, without naming the activities. For instance, say "I need everybody to stand shoulder-to-shoulder, in a straight line." All kids (even big kids called adults) enjoy games, even if they won't admit it!

Subtle Supervision

At any age, adult supervision is required for kid's parties. You don't have to be a nuisance. Twelve year olds don't much appreciate Moms or Dads peering over their shoulders at boy-girl dance parties, for instance. But you can be unobtrusively around and on hand when needed.

Do It Their Way

Once again, your child's idea of a great party might not match yours. But it's your *child's* birthday, not *yours*. Do it the birthday child's way!

PARTIES FOR TWINS & OTHER MULTIPLES

Double Duty, Double Fun

When it comes to planning birthday parties, parents of twins and other multiples have double duty and double fun. Although your children obviously share this day, their birthdays provide an opportunity to affirm each one's individuality, unique personality and identity.

Share a Party? Sometimes!

I encourage you to listen to your children's desires. Pre-schoolers often like to share a party. As the kids get older, they may prefer separate parties on separate days, each with his or her own friends. Even if they share a single birthday party, there are ways you can make the celebration special for each of them.

Often, well-meaning family and friends subconsciously lump multiples together as a collective entity. Perhaps you yourself refer to them as "the twins." I've heard stories from twins of deep resentment over shared parties and presents.

Sometimes people address a single card to "Michael and Ryan" or, even worse, "The Twins." Don't do it! Treat each one as the individual he or she is and ask your family and friends to do the same. In fact, insist on it!

Celebrate the Individual

Here are some ideas for making the birthday celebration special for each of your children:

- Ask each of your birthday children what he or she would like to receive. Respect each one's need for individuality and independence. Your children's friends are often good sources for gift ideas. Sometimes they're more tuned in to individual characteristics and interests than family members!

- Always, *always* give each child an individual card.

- If the children will be having a combined birthday party, plan it together, incorporating ideas from each child---for the invitations, the cake, the decorations, the games, everything!

- If your children are in preschool and they request it, let the teacher know you'd like them to celebrate their birthdays on their own days.

- Make sure you sing "Happy Birthday" and blow out candles separately for each of your multiples. That may mean separate candles on the same cake or separate cakes.

Remember that all this (from cakes to candles to presents) grows more important the older your multiples get. They'll become increasingly aware of their own possessions, choices and say so!

When Your Multiples Open Presents

Even though we want to emphasize celebrating the individual, don't do two separate present openings. The guests may lose interest and, before you know it, the ceremonies will turn into disorder and chaos. Instead, seat the birthday children in the center of a circle of their guests. Use one of the present-opening games and have the guests give both their presents when its their turn.

> *TIP:* If you're giving your multiples a large gift to share, also give each one a small, individual present.

Attending Other Kids' Parties

Another issue for multiples may arise when only one is invited to another child's birthday party. The friend's parents should not feel they have to invite both twins (triplets, quadruplets, etc.) when their child wishes to invite only one. If one child's feelings are hurt by not being invited, arrange to do something special together while his or her sibling is at the party. That way everyone feels important.

THE BASICS

The next three chapters, GET READY!, GET SET! and LET'S PARTY!! cover all the basics of giving parties from planning the when's, where's and how's, right down to sending the thank you notes. Sound boring? Nope! You'll find some surprising ideas for turning the ordinary into the extraordinary. You and your birthday child will have fun!

GET READY!
GET SET!
LET'S PARTY!!

GET READY!

Hmm...What Type of Party Will We Have?

The type of party I like and use most often is the traditional 1-1/2 to 2 hour theme party, held at home or at a park. You'll see some great examples of the parties kids love best in the THEME PARTIES KIDS LOVE section.

Slumber parties are another great option but are best reserved for kids ten years and older. The younger crowd tends to feel a little insecure about spending the night away from home.

I've always loved surprise parties but suggest you wait until your child's a teenager when he or she will be better able to appreciate the time and effort you put into organizing and conducting such an event just for them.

How About a Theme?

Kids never tire of repetition. They may have attended a Silly Slimy Yucky Mucky Party at a friend's house and want to do the same thing for their party. That's fine! Take your lead from your child and don't worry about copying someone else's idea. The theme may be the same, but the party will be in your child's honor. It will be *your* child's turn for the royal treatment.

You don't *have* to have a theme. A birthday party is a theme all by itself. But it can be fun to select a special theme. The choices are endless. Here are just a few ideas:

- A favorite movie. You can find theme merchandise and props in party supply stores, toy stores, even grocery stores for many of the movies released for children.

- A Super Hero or Heroine your child is interested in.

- Teddy bears are a great hit with the younger crowd. This is an especially nice theme for a birthday child who is inseparable from his or her teddy bear.

- How about a theme that capitalizes on your child's interests? Take note of the dramatic play your child engages in. How about a Beach Party for the budding marine biologist? Or a Rock 'n Roll Glitter Party for an upcoming actor or actress?

- If the birthday is near a holiday and your child really wants to, you can use the widely available holiday decorations, paper products and games to make party planning a breeze.

Should You Hire a Party Professional?

1. Figure out if your budget will allow this option. As with everything else, inflation has caused prices to go up. Shop around to learn what you can get for your money.

2. Here are a few of the many party services and entertainment options available:

   ☆ Clowns
   ☆ Magicians
   ☆ Puppet Shows
   ☆ Pony Rides
   ☆ Face Painting

3. Find the right person

4. Your friends will be your first and most reliable source for recommendations.

   • Check your neighborhood, church youth organization or parks and recreation department for teenagers or young adults who love to perform. They usually enjoy working with kids, don't charge as much as professionals and often do every bit as great a job.

   • If you're at a loss for leads, take a look at telephone book listings and newspaper classifieds. Be careful; anyone can advertise. Always call references. Make sure the person's worked with the age group and is familiar with their interests and attention span (or lack thereof).

Planning the Party Agenda

Your party will last 1-1/2 to 2 hours. You'll need to plan lots of activities to fill the time. Take a look at the THEME PARTIES KIDS LOVE section for some great, action-packed, kid-tested parties.

I usually start with a half hour of arts and crafts, continue with a mixer, go on to non-stop fun activities, cake and ice cream, present opening, then before you know it, the party's over!

You'll need to plan activities even if you hire a performer. Most performances last just 30 to 45 minutes. The kids will need to get up and *moving* as soon as the show's over.

Help, Please!

If you invite more than four guests, always arrange help ahead of time. The younger the kids, the more help you'll need. The ideal ratio is one adult to every four or five kids. Solicit help from spouses, friends, relatives or favorite babysitters.

If the event will be in a setting away from home, ask one of each guest's parents to attend. This is especially important if the children are younger than six. (If you ask parents to attend, please plan to feed them too!)

Often, ten to twelve year olds who love kids will jump at the chance to help with a party, especially if they get paid. I usually pay my young helpers a flat fee of $20 per party to make it worth their while. I never have a shortage of volunteers!

If you're asking a friend to help, offer a trade. They'll be glad of your help when it's their turn to give a birthday party.

When to Have the Party

The Best Days for Parties

Saturdays and Sundays are the best days for parties. Parties during the week often conflict with other scheduled activities and appointments. Depending on the age group, kids may be just too tired and irritable to enjoy a party after a long day at school.

Try to avoid conflicts with other parties, school activities and organized sports. It's disappointing for you and your birthday child when guests can't attend because of prior commitments.

> **PARTY ANIMAL TIP:**
>
> *If your child's birthday occurs during a school holiday or vacation, have the party before school lets out or after it starts up again. Be sure to keep the party separate from any holiday celebrations.*

I no longer do parties during holiday breaks and do very few parties during June, July and August because I've seen too many kids whose hearts were broken when only five of fifteen invited guests could attend.

The Best Times for a Party

The best times for parties depend on your child's age:

- If your child is three or younger, plan the party for before or after naps and meals. 11:00 am to 12:30 p.m. or 3:00 to 4:30 p.m. are usually good times.

- For ages four through nine, the prime times are 1:00 p.m. to 2:30 p.m. or 3:00 p.m.

- Older kids are more flexible. Just about any time will do!

If your child is three or younger, the party should not last longer than an hour and a half. Two hours is the max for any age group. The only exception would be if the party is going to be away from home and you need to allow travel time.

Before You Set the Date

Here's a checklist I follow when setting party dates:

❑   If you plan to use professional help, find out if the entertainers or party service providers will be available.

❑   Talk to your spouse, babysitter, friends, etc., to see who can help you on the date you have in mind.

❑   Call the parents of your child's best friends to make sure the intended guests can attend on that date. (Let them know you'll send a written invitation later.)

What's the Best Location for Your Party?

Will you have the party at your house or away from home? Indoors or outdoors?
Now's the time to decide.

Outdoors

My first choice party location is outdoors -- whether it's a
park, playground or your own backyard. Spills and
messes are minor instead of major tragedies. Plan a
backup in case the weather doesn't cooperate. A clean
garage or basement will do just fine.

Indoors

If you decide to have the party indoors, contain the
guests to one or two rooms. Keep the birthday child's
bedroom off limits. Otherwise guests may be tempted
to leave the party to play with your child's favorite toys.
Birthday parties work best when everyone joins in. Save
the bedroom for another day when your child has just
one friend over to play.

Good indoor activities include get-acquainted games
and present opening. Activities better done outdoors
include movement games, art experiences and
refreshments.

Family rooms make good birthday party sites. They're
often near the back patio or porch. I like to push the
coffee table and other furniture to the edge of the room
so I can go from active, outdoor play to indoor activities.

Away From Home

If you want to have the party away from home, make sure the location is appropriate for your child's and your guests' age. Remember, you're responsible and liable for all the children in your care.

Popular party destinations include:

☺ fast food restaurants,

☺ child-oriented pizza, hamburger or ice cream parlors,

☺ kindergyms, gymnastics centers and indoor play establishments,

☺ amusement and theme parks,

☺ parks, playgrounds and tot lots,

☺ ice and roller-skating rinks,

☺ miniature golf courses,

☺ bowling alleys,

☺ pre-schools (they'll sometimes rent out their facilities to members),

☺ children's museums, and

☺ entertainment centers.

No Movies, Puhleez!

For any party, any age group -- do *not* go to see a movie. Even if it's the latest, greatest, newest release, sitting in the dark and keeping quiet does *not* constitute a celebration.

The Guest List

Let the birthday child decide who he or she wants to invite. You may feel all the children who have invited your child to their parties should be included. I don't think this should be mandatory, especially if your child's not particularly close to those children. I do suggest you include any of your child's siblings, either as guests or as helpers.

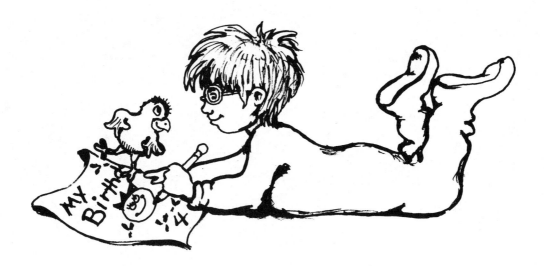

How Many Kids Should You Invite?

The old rule of thumb is to invite as many friends as the birthday child's age. I suggest letting the birthday child invite eight to fifteen guests of similar age for the most fun. That may sound like a lot of kids, but think of it this way: besides being a time for fun and play, a birthday party is also an opportunity to develop social awareness. (There! If you needed a reason to let loose, you've got it!) Parties help kids learn how to:

- Accept and enjoy others,
- Give as well as receive,
- Share and take turns,
- Use good manners, and
- Converse with each other and adults.

Consider Inviting a Friend to Stay

I recommend inviting the birthday child's best friend to stay after the party too, to share in the excitement. The birthday child will still be revved up and could use the companionship. You may need some time yourself to catch your breath and relax a bit.

But, I Didn't Invite Gerry's Brother

Don't assume you have to invite the siblings of the guests your child is inviting. You need to keep the number of guests at the party to a manageable number and you want those guests to be your child's friends. Don't feel shy about saying "no" if a parent asks if it would be okay for Gerry's brother to come too.

Invitation Ideas

I don't recommend writing out individual invitations for each guest. It's just too labor intensive! Instead, I suggest you...

- Have your child draw a picture on a piece of paper, perhaps relating to the party theme. Write the necessary information on the bottom, then take it down to your local copy center to make copies.

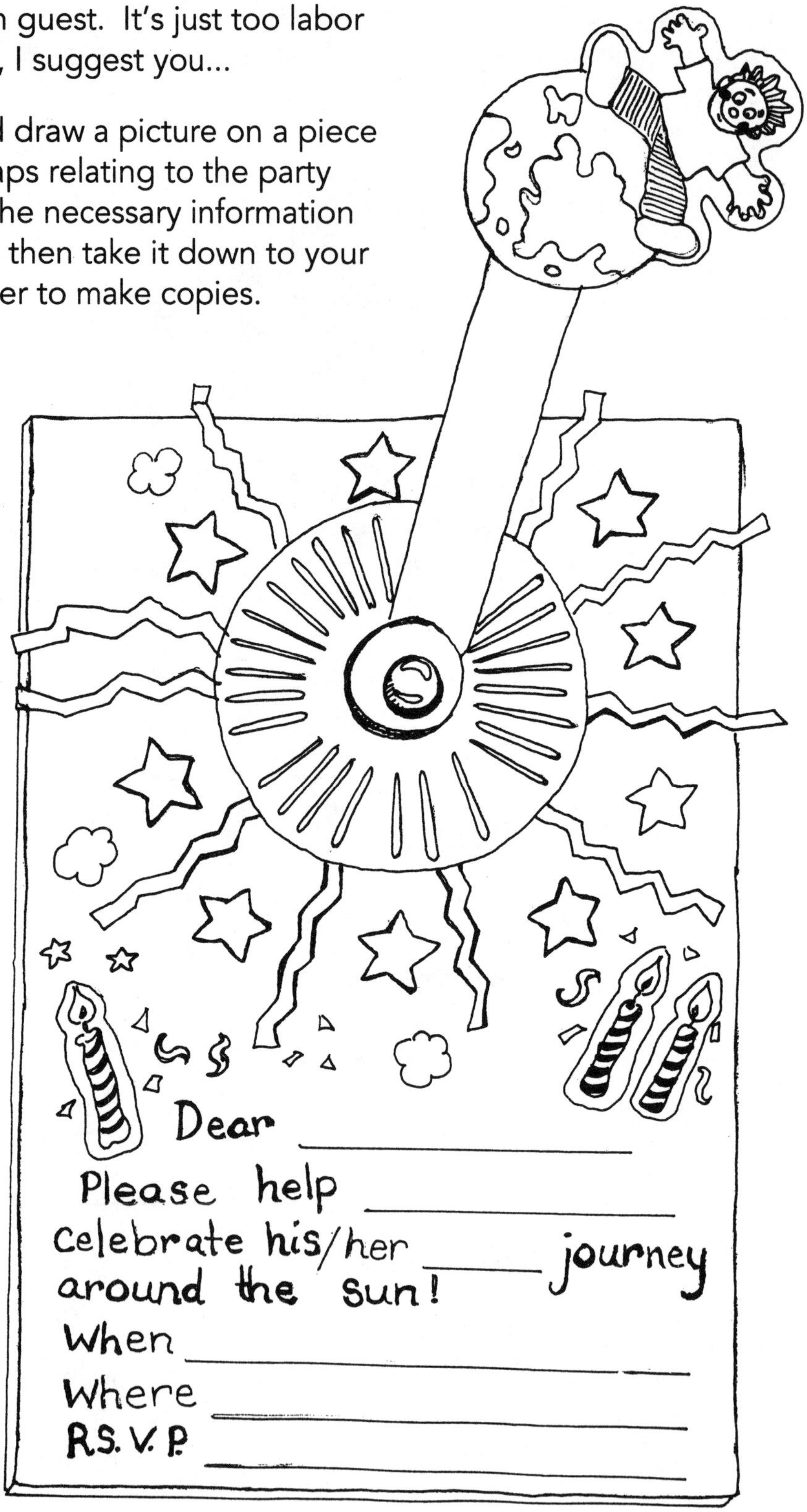

Dear _____

Please help _____

Celebrate his/her _____ journey

around the sun!

When _____

Where _____

R.S.V.P. _____

- Take your birthday child shopping with you and buy ready-made invitations. (You'll still have your work cut out filling in the blanks and addressing the invitations.)

- Or, Use your computer to make the invitations. Here's a fun example:

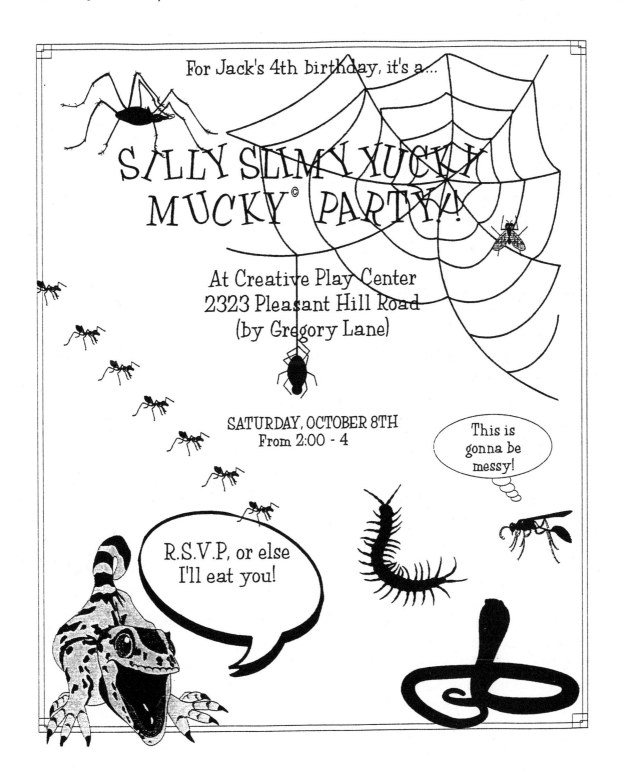

Invitation Checklist

Be sure to include the following information in the invitations:

❑ Who the party's for,

❑ The date, start and end times,

❑ Always, *always* an RSVP with your phone number and the date by which you need an answer.

Also, let your guests know whether...

❑ They should bring or wear special clothes (e.g., a swimsuit or play clothes),

❑ A meal will be served,

❑ You would like (or require) one or both parents or other responsible adults to attend the party,

❑ Guests will be transported to another location.

Distributing the Invitations

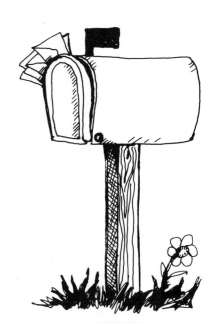

Send the invitations out three to four weeks in advance. There's nothing worse than a last minute invitation -- the recipient wonders if she or he's being invited as an afterthought or to fill in for someone higher up on the list who couldn't come, and the parents are inconvenienced by having to shop for a present on short notice.

Please use the postal system to mail the invitations. Avoid hurting feelings -- don't distribute invitations at school unless you plan to invite the entire class.

RSVP's -- a Must!

If you don't hear from the invited guests' parents by the date requested, call them up. Ask if they received the invitation. Tell them your birthday child would like to know whether his or her friend is coming. As the host, you need to know how many children will attend so you can plan refreshments, games, party bags, etc. The count will be critical for organizing as well as budgeting if you plan to hire an entertainer, provide pony rides or take guests to another location.

GET SET!

Decorations: Keep 'em Simple!

Don't spend a lot of time or money on decorations. I suggest you hang streamers or let the birthday child draw pictures to put around the party area (indoors or outdoors).

Let the birthday child (age 4 and up) help you decorate. Follow your child's lead. The process or "doing" is part of the fun and anticipation.

Balloons

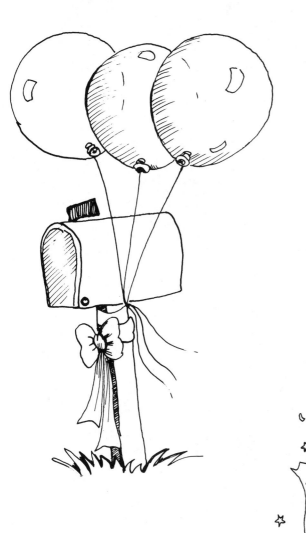

Balloons are fun and go hand in hand with parties. Tie a bunch to the mailbox to help guests find the party house. Tie a helium filled balloon to each guest's chair, to trees or to other indoor or outdoor furniture. After the party, guests may take the balloons home.

Be sure to buy or fill the helium balloons the day of the party; if you do it sooner, they'll lose their holding power. I don't recommend tying a bunch of balloons together as a centerpiece decoration unless you can figure out a way to keep them from tangling. (I never could.)

Prizes, Favors & Party Bags

Whether your child is two or nine, a party bag is a must. This is especially important for younger guests. Two year olds really cannot understand the concept of gift giving -- they want to keep and open the presents their parents have just wrapped for the birthday child. With party bags, *everyone* gets a gift.

If your child is four or older, go shopping together. Let your child select the toys and candy for the party bags. Popular favors include small toys, trinkets, bubble gum and small lollipops. The favors you and the birthday child select will vary depending on the age of the guests. Don't worry too much about the quality of the gifts and prizes; most small guests appreciate quantity more!

Party Hats and Blowers, No Thanks!

Party hats and blowers are optional. I find them frustrating for adults as well as children. Not all children want to wear the hats and the rubber bands inevitably break on some of them. The adults end up scrambling to fix hats while they try to light the candles on the cake at the same time.

Blowers are often poorly constructed. If you decide to use them, be sure to have extras on hand because many won't work properly. Also, you'll need to have the children get the blowers out of their mouths (which might not be easy if they're tootling away while you're trying to talk to them), so they can sing "Happy Birthday."

Prize Chests

You can assemble party bags ahead of time or fill a prize chest (a cooler, box or other container will work fine) with an assortment of small toys and candy. Let the guests pick a specified number of items from the prize chest to put in their party bags. If the birthday child is five, for example, let each guest pick five toys and five candies. Children really enjoy the power of choice.

Catalog Shopping (a Timesaver!)

I do all my party favor shopping from catalogs. Be sure to place your order at least a couple of weeks before the party. It's easy to acquire a catalog by calling the toll free numbers. Here are three of my favorites:

FOR ART SUPPLIES

Discount School Supply
P.O. Box 670
Capitola, California 95010-0670
1-800-627-2829

FOR PARTY FAVORS
(And Some Art Supplies)

Oriental Trading Co., Inc.
P. O. Box 3407
Omaha, Nebraska 68103-0408
1-800-228-2269

U. S. Toy Co., Inc.
1227 East 119th Street
Grandview, Missouri 64030-0475
1-800-255-6124

Party Bag Alternatives

- Many of the art creations described for the theme parties are party favors in and of themselves.

- You may want to give each guest one larger item as an alternative to a party bag. One parent I know gave out cowboy hats and bandannas at her son's pony riding party.

- Kids like this unique party favor: Use a Polaroid camera to take a photo of each guest with the birthday child. Put the photo in a frame which you and your child made ahead of time.

Have the birthday child hand out the party bags at the end of the party as the guests walk out the door. Encourage guests to wait to look in their party bags until they get home (or in the car on their way home). This way they won't lose or break their favors or leave candy wrappers for you to clean up!

Piñatas

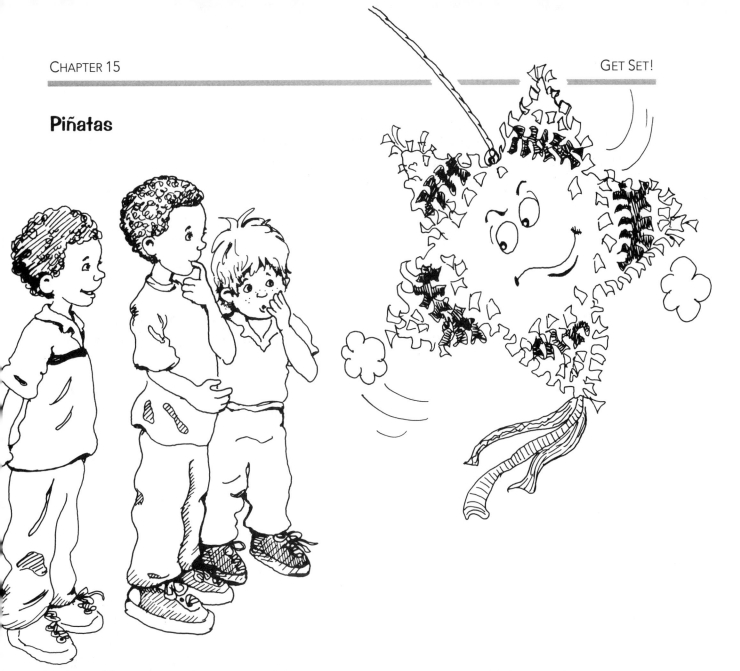

I don't like piñatas because of the competitive, aggressive behavior that results: from hitting the piñata to grabbing the candy or treats. But, if a piñata is a tradition and a must for your child's party, please consider the following suggestions:

1. Fill small plastic sandwich bags with identical amounts of candy and favors. Make one for each child at the party including the birthday child.

2. Let the guests know there's one bag for each child. This keeps one child from "hogging" all the prizes and prevents the possibility of tears from children who receive few, if any, treats in the usual wild, candy-grabbing stampede.

3.   Purchase or make a piñata that can break open easily. Don't try to save the piñata from year to year. You might enjoy trying one of the new piñatas that has strings the guests pull to dispense the prizes. (Great idea!)

4.   Inform the guests of the rules for playing the piñata game:

- They are to stay in line, standing shoulder-to-shoulder so they can all see, except when it's their turn to hit the piñata.

- They are not to run out until all the contents have spilled out and you give them the go ahead.

5.   Do not blindfold the child who is trying to hit the piñata. Young children are usually afraid of blindfolds. Even older children may be uncomfortable with them.

6.   An adult often needs to help out to break open the piñata and disperse the contents. Children usually don't mind the adult stepping in as they get tired of waiting.

Once all the contents are on the ground, give the kids permission to rush in and each take one bag of goodies.

Paper Products

Buy disposable paper products for safe handling and easy cleanup. If you're doing a theme party, look to see if the paper goods are available for the theme. Otherwise, use the birthday child's favorite color.

I recommend you buy plastic spoons, but no forks. The spoons can be used for both cake and ice cream.

Refreshments, Yum!

Simple Is Better

Nutritionists tell us never to skip a meal, but I want to convince you not to serve a meal or even put out snack foods at the birthday party. Some parents think they'll kill more time by serving lunch or dinner. This isn't necessarily true: some kids won't eat anyway! Either they won't like what you're serving, or they'll be too excited to eat.

Kids usually grab snacks by the handful and eat them on the run. This creates a safety hazard -- kids can easily choke if they're eating while playing -- and a mess. I encourage you to have the children eat and drink just once during the party: right after singing "Happy Birthday."

Ya Gotta Do What Ya Gotta Do

If you feel you *must* serve food, arrange to have cheese pizzas delivered. Hardly any kid will turn down a cheese pizza, and what a treat when the doorbell rings and there's a special delivery just for the birthday child.

The Cake, the Cake, the Very Important Cake!

You can help your birthday child make a cake from scratch or from a cake mix. This could be a ritual you establish in your family. On the other hand, if either of you doesn't *like* making cakes, don't do it. A commercially made cake the birthday child picks out can be just the ticket to making you both happy.

Don't go out and spend a lot of money on a cake. Grocery store bakeries do as good a job, if not better, than the most expensive bakeries in town. Let the birthday child pick out exactly what she or he wants -- from flavor, filling and frosting to the decorations on top.

As a cake connoisseur, sometimes sampling up to five cakes a week, I've developed a taste for fresh cake. One of my pet peeves is the cake made with frosting you can't even wash off your hands. You know the kind I mean. It's made with whipped shortening and sugar. It leaves a greasy film on your fingers. Yech. Of course, if your birthday child requests it...

If you want the freshest cake in town, order one with a whipped cream frosting or a pudding or custard filling. There's no way this cake can be made ahead of time and frozen. (I've found some bakeries do just that with a sheet cake. They pull it out of the freezer on the morning you plan to pick it up, then frost and decorate it.)

Some parents think carrot cake is a wholesome choice. The fact is, most kids don't like the texture and it's full of oil, too. Stick to your child's favorite or basic chocolate or vanilla.

But Ma, I Don't Like Cake.

What if your child doesn't like cake? No problem. How about...

- **Cookies!** Have your child help you make his or her favorite cookies. You'll be able to stick candles into them just fine. Chocolate chip cookies are the most frequent request. You can make them way ahead of time and store them in the freezer. I've never witnessed any waste when chocolate chip cookies were served. Guests ask for more, more, more!!

- **Cupcakes!** If you serve cupcakes instead of cake, adorn one cupcake with the appropriate number of candles and serve it to the birthday child first. I've seen too many birthdays where parents put only one candle on the cupcake. It's easier for the parents, but not as much fun for the birthday child.

- **Or...Let Them Eat Ice Cream!** -- Ice cream cake or frozen yogurt pie makes a great alternative to cake, especially if your child is more of an ice cream lover than a cake eater. At our house, ice cream cake was the traditional "cake." Of course, the birthday child must pick his or her favorite flavor of ice cream or frozen yogurt!

Ice Cream

If you're serving cake, cupcakes or cookies, offer ice cream too. Let the birthday child pick the flavor. You may think it should be chocolate or vanilla, but if the birthday child says mint chip or orange sherbet, go for it. Remember, this is the one special day when your child gets to make *all* the choices!

An Old Party Animal Trick:

This foolproof idea eliminates the struggle of scooping hard ice cream or the mess of soft ice cream.

1. Scoop the ice cream into cupcake liners placed in a cupcake or muffin tin.

2. Place the pan in the freezer several hours or a day or two before the party.

3. Take the pan out of the freezer at cake cutting time. Voila! Instant, easy scoops of ice cream.

If you feel you *must* offer the guests a choice of flavors, scoop vanilla ice cream into half the cupcake liners and your child's favorite flavor into the other half.

Another way to simplify serving ice cream is to buy individual ice cream cups in bulk.

Beverages

The one beverage I've never seen kids turn down is Cherry 7 Up. It has no caffeine and it doesn't stain. It's "beyond" apple juice in that it appeals to older children.

Another good choice is milk. Nothing goes better with cake. (Do you suppose all those commercials have gotten to me?)

Or, how about water? None of us seems to drink enough of it, including our children. In fact, even if you serve soda, juice or milk, also serve water. Make it available throughout the course of the party. There's nothing like water for quenching thirst.

TIP:

- *Use paper cups,*
- *Fill the cups only half full (guests can always ask for more)*
- *Take the beverage to the guests*

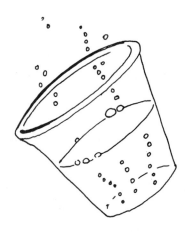

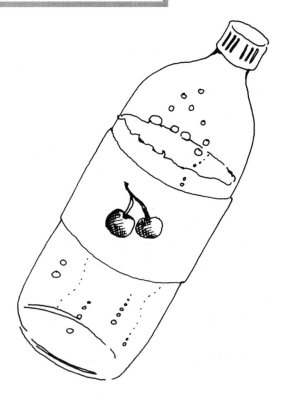

Sugar Highs?

A birthday party is not a good time to be overly zealous about nutrition. Cake, ice cream and sugary foods get the blame for causing children to become hyperactive at parties but recent research indicates sugar does not increase aggressiveness or physical activity in children. Just anticipating the big event or being at the birthday party is a high in itself.

What if Bobby's Allergic?

Check on guests with food allergies. Many children are allergic to chocolate, dairy products and nuts. Most parents will relay this information to you when they RSVP. It's their responsibility to bring a food substitute, not yours.

LET'S

DON'T TOUCH!

There are certain parts of a party which I do pretty much the same way, tradition and fun. Serving the cake is the highlight of any birthday party.

PARTY!

perhaps with slight variations, every time. The kids count on and love the
Keep reading for details.

High Drama~Serving the Cake.

Here's the ceremony I use to serve the cake:

Set the Stage

1. Seat the guests around the tablecloth which you've placed on the ground or a table. Serve each guest a half cup of Cherry 7-Up or another beverage. Refill as necessary.

2. Walk around with the cake to let each guest preview it. This satisfies everyone's curiosity, not just the few sitting near the birthday child. Everyone wants to see what the cake looks like and the birthday child will be pleased to show off the cake he or she picked out or helped make.

3. Have the birthday child put the candles on the cake. This builds your child's self-esteem by giving him or her a sense of pride and ownership in the party.

4. If you're indoors, ask the birthday child if she or he would like the lights on or off when blowing out the candles. Most three year olds want the lights on, while five year olds must have the lights off.

Begin the Play!

5.   As you light the candles, count each one in unison with the guests. If you've added a candle to "grow on," light it after you've finished lighting the other candles and say "and one to grow on."

6.   Lead the guests in singing a rousing "Happy Birthday." Suggest the birthday child make a wish before blowing out the candles.

7.   Whoosh! There they go...the birthday child blows out the candles!

8. Give the birthday child permission to lick the frosting off the candles and the decorations. Let the birthday child keep the decorations.

9. Take the cake to a nearby counter. Cut small pieces to avoid waste. The guests can always ask for more.

10. Serve it with the pre-scooped ice cream.

11. Bring the cake and/or ice cream to the guests seated at the table or around a table cloth placed on the grass or patio.

12. Explain to the guests (if they're not used to this tradition) that they must wait for the birthday child to take the first bite before they begin eating.

13. Serve the birthday child first, then the other guests.

14. After all the guests have been served, the birthday child takes the first bite to signal that everyone may begin eating.

PARTY ANIMAL TIP:

If guests start asking for a certain piece of birthday cake (e.g., the one with the flower on it), remind them that they're guests at the party and will eat what they're served. It's okay if they want only ice cream and no cake. Just make sure you don't end up being a short order chef, catering to each guest's individual desires.

Break Down the Set!

When the children have finished eating, ask them to clear their places. Have them pour any liquid left in their cups into the sink (or an empty bucket if you're outdoors). Provide trash cans or bags and ask them to throw paper products and leftovers away before leaving the eating area.

Opening Presents~The Center of Attention!

Opening presents is a must at every birthday party. Sometimes it's the first thing the birthday child wants to do. I refrain from beginning the party with present opening as a courtesy to guests who may arrive late. I believe it's important to get the guests involved in the activities of the party itself first -- whether those are painting, making party bags or stringing necklaces.

Designate a Special Spot

As guests arrive, designate a place for them to put their presents such as a table, sofa, or corner of the family room. Even a laundry basket or empty box will work.

"Open Mine!   Open Mine First!"

How many parties have you attended where guests shove the presents into the birthday child's lap and make present opening a popularity contest or even a competitive activity? Manners are virtually lost and barbaric uncivilized tendencies take over as children lose it all in a present opening frenzy.

Many parents want to skip the present opening altogether for this very reason. But, think how disappointed the guests would be. To ignore their gifts might cause hurt feelings.

Make It a Game

If you follow a few simple guidelines, opening presents can be great fun. I suggest making it a game which involves everyone. You'll need the following materials:

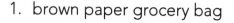

PRESENT OPENING GAME MATERIALS

1. brown paper grocery bag

2. a toy or stuffed animal chosen by the birthday child

3. tape recorder or CD player

4. cassette tape or CD with the birthday child's favorite song

5. children's scissors (for cutting stubborn ties)

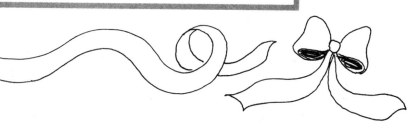

Ready? Here we go...

Explain the rules of the present opening game to the guests and the birthday child before you begin.

1.   Ask the guests to sit in a circle with their gifts behind their backs.

2.   Seat the birthday child in the middle of the circle.

3.   An adult or sibling helper turns the music on.

> While the music plays, the guests pass the toy chosen by the birthday child around the circle.

> When it stops, the guest who is holding the toy gives his or her present to the birthday child.

4.   The birthday child reads (or is read) the card, opens the present then, after admiring it, passes it to you.

5.   An adult helper records who gave what gift. This makes the task of writing thank you notes much easier.

6.   Hold the present up so everyone can see it. Explain that presents will not be taken apart, assembled, passed around or played with at this time.

7.   Put the present to the side for the birthday child to play with after the guests leave. Put the wrapping paper in the brown paper bag.

8.   Before the music starts again, the birthday child makes eye contact with the guest who gave the present and says "Thank you." This is easy to remember as that guest is still holding the toy or stuffed animal.

9.   After the guest says "You're welcome," the music starts again and the guests continue passing the toy or stuffed animal around the circle.

10.   The present opening game ends when all the guests have given their gifts.

This game is an all time favorite and, I might add, makes present opening a smooth and pleasurable experience for kids and adults every time. You'll find variations in the THEME PARTIES KIDS LOVE section.

It's Time to Say Goodbye

When a Guest Must Leave Early

If a guest has to leave before the present opening game, ask the guest to retrieve her or his present from the pile and give it to the birthday child. Have the birthday child open the gift in front of the guest and, of course, say "Thank you" for the present.

Parents Arrive

Parents will start to arrive to pick up their children as you finish up the last activity of the party -- opening presents. Parents will be amazed to witness the orderly and organized present opening game. They'll wonder if the party was always so calm (of course it was!) and how you did it.

Out of Sight, Out of Mind!

Gather up and put away the presents the birthday child received. This eliminates the opportunity for curious guests to talk the birthday child into playing with the presents and possibly breaking them or losing some parts. Let the birthday child be the first one to take the presents out of their packages and play with them.

Don't Forget Your Party Bags!

There will always be some parents who are a little late picking up their kids. Let any kids who are waiting for rides have some unstructured time playing in the yard or family room. As parents or carpools arrive, remind guests to retrieve their party bags and any wonderful creations from Make 'n Create.

Thank You For Coming to the Best Party <u>Ever</u>!

As each guest leaves, the birthday child thanks him or her individually for coming to the *best party ever!*

Whew! The Party's Over

Now what? Perhaps you feel relieved that it's over for yet another year. Give yourself a pat on the back -- you did it! You should be proud of the gift you've given your child and your family: the *best party ever* and memories which will be cherished for years.

If your child hasn't invited a friend to stay, you may want to spend some time together looking at the new presents, perhaps reading a new book your child received, assembling a new toy or playing a new game. Or, you may want to help your birthday child put the presents away in his or her room.

Be prepared for your child to feel let down after everyone's gone home. This would be a good time to watch it if you've made a video tape of the big event.

Thank You's

It's a nice idea to send a thank you note for gifts, but a hard one to follow through with. Here are some suggestions and a sample thank you card. You're welcome to duplicate it for your own use.

A Little Help's In Order

If your child's writing skills are still under development, you may want to write down your child's thoughts exactly as dictated to you. Then, let your child sign or write his or her initial on the note.

Fun Photo Thank You

A thank you photo is a fun alternative to a traditional thank you note. Prepare simple cardboard or fabric frames a week or two before the party. This is a great activity for you and your birthday child to do together.

On the day of the party ask an adult helper to take a Polaroid picture of each guest with the birthday child when the guest arrives. Then the adult helper can assemble the photos in the frames so they're ready to go home after the party.

The photos serve two purposes in one: They make great party favors and wonderful thank you notes!

THEME PARTIES
KIDS LOVE

The theme parties in this book are organized according to age. If your child fits into the age group, you can be sure the games and activities are appropriate for the age and developmental level. Even if your child's a little older than the specified age group, don't worry about the games being too simple. You'll be surprised at how much older children enjoy all the games and activities, no matter what age level is specified.

I've tried to make the games and activities shown for each theme party unique, but all of them can be adapted for any theme. There are just three things to remember when it comes to selecting games and activities:

✳ Both you and your child should be comfortable with them,

✳ Keep the tempo lively and upbeat, and

✳ Above all, have fun!

PARTY ANIMAL TIP: If a game is successful one year, play it again in subsequent years. Kids love tradition, especially since they get better and better each time they play a game. Repetition helps us learn - no matter what our age!

BACKYARD

BEACH PARTY

You don't have to travel to a beach to host this party -- your own backyard is the perfect spot for fun in the sun -- even if you don't have a swimming pool! A hose or sprinkler should be available as well as a wading pool, then you're ready to *get all wet*. I've included many activity choices so you can select those that best fit your party and your child's age and wishes.

Backyard Beach Party Snapshot

AGES:	**4 TO 8**
TOTAL TIME:	**1-1/2 TO 2 HOURS**

30 minutes	**Make 'n Create** Party Bags Bubble Prints Beach Collage Squirt Bottle Painting
15-20 minutes	**Get-Together Time** Beach Ball Name Ball Beach Day Take Away Sea Shell Hunt
20-30 minutes	**Games & Activities** Musical Beach Balls/Balloons Partner Beach Balls/Balloons Water Balloon Toss Penny Dive Jump the Stream
15 minutes	**Let's Eat!** Cake Popsicles Ice Cold Drinks
15-20 minutes	**Open Presents** Catch a Ducky or Shark Attack

Get Ready!

Invitations

Ask your guests to bring swimsuits and towels.

Checklists

Party Bags

- ❑ white paper lunch bags
- ❑ watercolor markers/crayons
- ❑ summer fun stickers and/or rubber stamps (shells, sea-life, etc..)
- ❑ stamp pads (washable, non-toxic)
- ❑ prizes geared to the age of the guests: inflatable beach balls, squirt toys, sand toys, bottles of bubbles, plastic sunglasses, sugarless bubble gum, small toy boats, small plastic marine life creatures, sidewalk chalk, pinwheels, assortment of individually wrapped candy, etc.
- ❑ small cooler, box or container for "prize chest"

Supplies & Decorations

- ❑ paper products (tablecloth, plates, cups, napkins)
- ❑ plastic products (forks)
- ❑ balloons/streamers (optional)
- ❑ wading pool, hose and sprinkler
- ❑ plastic tablecloths, old blankets or sheets

Bubble Prints

- ❑ food coloring or Liquid Watercolor (red, yellow, blue)
- ❑ 3 small plastic bottles of bubbles
- ❑ white paper (art, copy or computer)
- ❑ permanent marker

Beach Collage

- ❏ jug or bottles of white craft glue (my favorite is Elmer's Glue-All)

- ❏ pieces of 8 1/2" x 11" cardboard or matte board (free from a frame shop just for the asking)

- ❏ several cardboard cartons/trays (the type that hold four 6-packs of canned soda)

- ❏ some of the following: sand, shells, pebbles, colored aquarium gravel or art rock, dried seaweed, small pieces of driftwood

- ❏ marker

TIP:

If you have a large jug of glue, pour it into paper bowls and supply the kids with popsicle or craft sticks for applying it.

Squirt Bottle Painting

- ❏ 1 or 2 paint-with-water books

- ❏ 2-3 spray bottles with adjustable nozzles

- ❏ clothesline for hanging pictures (or you can use your backyard fence)

- ❏ bag of clothespins

- ❏ permanent marker

Get-Together Time

- ❏ 1 inflatable beach ball

- ❏ 5-10 summer, water or beach type items, e.g., sun glasses, sun screen, small toy boat, fish, duck, sea shell, squirt toy, bottle of bubbles, sand shovel and bucket

- ❏ scarf or bandanna

- ❏ enough assorted sea shells (collect or buy) so each guest may find as many as the birthday child is old.

Games & Activities

- ❑ 9" or 11" latex, helium quality balloons or inflatable beach balls. (one for each guest plus extras.)
- ❑ Beach Boys music
- ❑ CD/tape player
- ❑ 1-2 bags of water balloons
- ❑ pennies (enough for each guest to find as many as the age of the birthday child, plus a few extras)

Refreshments

- ❑ cake -- make or purchase according to the birthday child's wishes
- ❑ box of popsicles or any ice cream bars on sticks
- ❑ jug of lemonade or cooler of soft drinks
- ❑ large plastic trash bag

Present Opening

Get supplies for *one* of these two fun present opening games:

Catch A Ducky
- ❑ butterfly or fishing net
- ❑ plastic ducks (make sure they float in water)

Shark Attack
- ❑ inflatable shark or stuffed toy shark
- ❑ Jimmy Buffett or Beach boys music
- ❑ CD/tape player
- ❑ paper trash bag
- ❑ children's scissors

Don't Forget

- ❑ candles and matches
- ❑ camera
- ❑ video camera
- ❑ film
- ❑ 3-4 helpers (spouse, older siblings, relatives, teenagers, friends)
- ❑ portable CD/tape player
- ❑ back-up batteries for CD/tape player and cameras

Get Set!

The Day Before the Party:

- ❑ Make the cake (if that was your child's choice)
- ❑ Add food coloring or Liquid Watercolor to the three bottles of bubbles (one color per bottle). Make sure there is a bubble blower wand in each bottle.

The Day of the Party:

- ❑ Decorate the party area (optional)
- ❑ Pick up the birthday cake if you ordered one.
- ❑ Fill the cooler, box or container with the toys and assorted candies you bought for prizes --stir it up with fingers. Now you have a prize chest!
- ❑ Spread out plastic tablecloths, blankets or sheets and set out supplies (refer to the checklist above) for the Make 'n Create areas:
  - ❁ party bag making
  - ❁ bubble prints
  - ❁ beach collage
  - ❁ squirt bottle painting

❑ For the Squirt Bottle Painting area: fill spray bottles with water, adjust the nozzles so water squirts out in a single stream. Tear the pictures out of the paint-with-water books. Set the materials near a fence or clothesline, with clothespins nearby.

❑ Decide where you'll hold the Get-Together Time and the Present Opening games. You'll need space to spread out a sheet or blanket for everyone to sit around.

❑ Get the yard ready for games and activities. You'll need open space to move around in. Pick up toys and check to make sure you haven't missed any mementos left by your pets.

❑ Set a table for refreshments or decide where you'll put a tablecloth on the ground. (This is what I like to do.)

❑ Fill water balloons (at least one for every two children --have extras.)

❑ Blow up beach balls or balloons.

❑ Fill wading pool with water. Make sure a nearby hose is connected and ready to re-fill the pool if needed.

❑ Make a jug of lemonade or punch. Also have ice cold water available. It's a must and the best thirst quencher!

Let's Party!

Station helpers at the Make 'n Create areas. When guests arrive, send them to the Party Bag making area. *After guests finish each project, direct them to the prize chest to pick a prize and a piece of candy and put them in their party bags. Place the party bag behind the prize chest, then send them to the next Make 'n Create area.* Keep the tempo fast and fun!

Make 'n Create

Party Bags

1. Give each guest a flat white lunch bag.

2. Helper or guest writes guest's name on the front of the bag.

3. Guest decorates the bag.

Bubble Prints

Ask each guest to write his or her name on a piece of white paper with a marker. (Provide help or do it for them if needed.) Explain how to make a bubble print picture by following this process:

1. Dip bubble blowing wand into the colored bubble solution.

2. Blow bubbles onto the white paper.

3. Watch bubbles pop and leave an imprint.

4. Try the other colored bubble solutions.

5. Cover the entire surface of the paper with popped bubbles.

6. Put the completed bubble print picture in a safe spot to dry.

> TIP: Don't get too close or it might sting your eyes!

Beach Collage

Give each guest a cardboard tray with a piece of matte board or cardboard in it and ask the guest to:

1. Write his or her name on the back of the matte board or cardboard.

2. Create a design or scene by gluing the collage materials to the matte board or cardboard.

3. Put the beach collage in a safe place to dry.

Squirt Bottle Painting

*   Let the guest select a "paint-with-water" picture.

*   Ask the guest to write his or her name on the picture with a marker. Help the guest if writing skills are still under development.

*   Hang the picture on a clothesline or fence with clothespins.

*   Now, ask the guest to take a spray bottle and squirt water at the picture until it is "painted."

Get-Together Time

Spread out a blanket or sheet and gather the guests into a circle, sitting around the edge. Begin with the Beach Ball Name Game to find out the names of all the guests who came to your child's birthday party.

While the Beach Ball Name Game's going on, have a helper hide sea shells for the Sea Shell Hunt in an area of the yard not visible to guests. If you have a sandbox, why not just bury the shells in it.? Bury them along the edges and not too deeply or the kids will become frustrated when they can't find the shells easily.

Beach Ball Name Ball

1. Place an inflated beach ball on the ground in front of you.
2. Instruct the kids to say their names when the ball rolls to them.
3. Start the game by rolling the ball to the birthday child.

4. The birthday child says his or her name.
5. Comment on how old the birthday child is on this birthday and say "We're all here today to celebrate _____'s birthday."
6. The birthday child rolls the ball to one of the guests.
7. The guest says his or her name out loud, then rolls the ball to someone who hasn't had a turn yet.
8. Continue Name Ball until everyone has had a turn.

Beach Day Take Away

1. Still sitting in a circle, show the guests the summer, beach theme items. Place them on the ground in front of you and name each one separately.

2. Put out as many items as the birthday child is old plus one more.

3. Cover all the items with the "magic" scarf or bandanna.

4. Instruct the guests to say the magic words while they wave one hand in front of them. (The magic words can be "Hocus Pocus Alamagocus" or any other "magic" words the guest of honor thinks of.)

5. Say the words along with the kids and on the last syllable, remove one or the items as you pick up the scarf. Don't let the guests see what you've removed!

6. Ask the guests if they can guess what's missing? Return item to its original spot.

7. Continue the game by waving two hands (stronger magic) over the scarf and removing 2 or more items when you say the magic words.

8. Once again, ask guests --different ones this time --to name the missing items.

9. On the final wave over the scarf (using the strongest magic of all), shake both of your hands while saying the magic words. Remove all the items as you lift up the scarf.

10. Ask the guests who've not had a turn to name the missing items.

11. The game ends when all the objects have been named. Lead the guests in giving themselves (and you!) a round of applause.

> TIP: If you're uncomfortable directing an activity, ask one of your helpers...it might be an activity he or she would really enjoy leading.

Sea Shell Hunt

1. Ask guests to retrieve their party bags from behind the prize chest and return to the Get-Together Time circle.

2. Show guests a sampling of the sea shells that are hidden in a special area for the Sea Shell Hunt.

3. Instruct the guests to find as many shells as the birthday child is old (e.g., four shells if Corrie is four years old). Demonstrate by counting out the number of shells they are to find.

4. Have the birthday child lead the guests to the Sea Shell Hunt area.

5. Instruct the guests to put the shells they find in their party bags and, when they've found the number of shells you've specified, show them to a helper.

6. Now, of course, send them on another trip to the prize chest to pick a prize and a piece of candy.

Games & Activities

Intersperse these games before and after refreshments and present opening. But, make sure you do at least one or two of before sitting down to eat.

Musical Beach Balls/Balloons

This game can be played indoors or outdoors (if it's not windy) with balloons. If there's even a slight breeze, beach balls work better and, of course, fit right in with the theme.

PARTY ANIMAL TIP:

Be sure to provide adult supervision whenever children are playing with balloons.

Give each guest an inflated balloon or beach ball. If you have a variety of colors, let each guest pick out a favorite and blow it up (provide help if needed).

Let the guests write (or, again, help if needed) their names on the balloons or beach balls with a permanent marker. Tell them they'll get to take the balloons or beach balls home as party prizes.

With your CD/tape player in hand and a rockin' Beach Boys song picked out, ask the guests to sit in a circle as the birthday child demonstrates how to play the game.

1. When the music starts, the guests stand up and keep the balloons or beach balls up in the air using only their hands.

2. When the music stops, the guests catch their balloons or beach balls and sit down right where they are.

3. The game continues this way with the starting and stopping of music and the children standing and sitting as the music indicates.

4. Provide further challenges by asking the guests to keep the balloons or beach balls up in the air with different body parts: one finger, two fingers, an elbow, a knee, a foot, their heads, etc. Be creative!

5. The game ends when the song is over.

Partner Beach Ball/Balloons

1. Each guest finds a partner.
2. The partners move around the open space, keeping the balloon or beach ball between them without using their hands.
3. Ask the birthday child to demonstrate the game with a partner.
4. Add variety to the game by stopping the music every once in awhile and challenging the participants to use different body parts, e.g.,
   - head to head,
   - arm to arm,
   - chest to chest,
   - back to back,
   - side to side,
   - knee to knee, and
   - tummy to tummy.

   The game begins when the music starts and ends when the music stops. Get ready for giggles!

Water Balloon Toss

1. Guests pair up (with someone different than before) and stand toe to toe with their partners, this forms two lines.

2. Give each of the guests in one line a water filled balloon.

3. Instruct the guests with the balloons to hand them to their partners on the word "toss."

4. Direct the guests who are now holding the balloons to take one step backward.

5. On the word "toss" the guests holding the balloons toss them to their partners. Suggest to the guests that underhand throws work best.

6. Continue the game, with the guests holding the balloons stepping backward then, on the word "toss," throwing the balloons to their partners.

7. If a balloon bursts at any time during the game, send the partners to the prize chest to pick a prize and a piece of candy to put in their party bags. Instruct them to return to the game and be an audience until the last pair's balloon bursts.

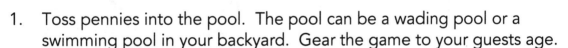

Penny Dive

1. Toss pennies into the pool. The pool can be a wading pool or a swimming pool in your backyard. Gear the game to your guests age.

2. Instruct the guests to find as many pennies as the birthday child is old. (For example, If your child is eight and there are ten children at the party, you'll need at least 80 pennies if each guest is to find 8. It's always a good idea to have extras.)

3. The younger set picks up the pennies from the bottom of the wading pool while; older kids who are good swimmers can dive to the bottom of a swimming pool.

4. Have children dry the pennies with their towels, then place them in their party bags.

> *Remember! Pools and all water activities require adult supervision.*

Jump the Stream

Form the guests into a circle. An adult or helper squats down in the center of the circle holding a water hose.

1. When the water is turned on, the adult turns slowly around keeping the stream of water close to the ground.

2. Tell children that when the stream of water gets close to them they are to jump to avoid getting wet.

3. Each time the adult completes a full revolution, he or she begins to turn a little bit faster and raises the stream slightly off the ground.

The object of the game is to stay dry but the most fun is to get squirted by the hose and, of course, get very wet!!

Let's Eat!

Refer to the *"High Drama~Serving the Cake"* section in the LET'S PARTY! chapter for the basics. Instead of serving ice cream in cups, hand out popsicles or ice cream bars.

Open Presents

Let your child choose one of these two present opening games.

Shark Attack

Follow the basic present opening procedure in the *"Opening Presents~The Center of Attention!"* section of the LET'S PARTY! chapter but use an inflated shark or stuffed toy shark to pass around to music selected from a Jimmy Buffett or Beach Boys CD or tape.

Catch a Ducky

1. Write each guest's name on the bottom of a plastic duck with a permanent marker.
2. Float the plastic ducks in a wading pool or swimming pool.
3. Ask the guests to retrieve the presents they brought.
4. Seat the guests near the pool.
5. The birthday child catches a ducky with a butterfly or fishing net and reads the name written on the bottom of the ducky.
6. The guest gives his or her present to the birthday child.
7. The birthday child gives the guest the ducky to keep as a party favor.
8. The birthday child opens the present and thanks the guest then catches the next ducky.

The Party's Over!

Send the guests home with their party bags, Make 'N Create projects, balloons or beach balls, duckies (if you played Catch a Ducky) and their towels. As the guests leave, the birthday child bids each one farewell and thanks him or her for coming.

Prince & Princess Party

Kings and Queens and Princes too
Want to wish you all that's new.
Which day? What day? What do you say? A birthday!
Happy Birthday to you!

Enter the world of Fantasyland. Your backyard becomes a magical kingdom as your child's favorite movie and fairy tale characters come to life. Prince Charming, Cinderella, Snow White, Princess Jasmine, Sleeping Beauty, King Arthur, Indian Princess Pocahontas...

Prince & Princess Party Snapshot

AGES:	**4 TO 8**
TOTAL TIME:	**1-1/2 TO 2 HOURS**
30 minutes	**Make 'n Create** Party Bags Crowns Necklaces
15-20 minutes	**Get-Together Time** "Mirror, Mirror" Hidden Jewels Ring & Bracelet Hunt
20-30 minutes	**Games & Activities** Magic Wand Dancing Royal Parade Lost Gold Knights & Dragons
15-20 minutes	**Let's Eat!** Cake Ice Cream Cherry 7-Up
15-20 minutes	**Open Presents** When You Wish Upon a Star

Get Ready!

Party Bags

- ❑ white paper lunch bags
- ❑ watercolor markers/crayons
- ❑ stickers (stars, etc., related to theme)
- ❑ rubber stamps and ink pads (washable/child safe)
- ❑ prize chest -- small cooler or any box or container
- ❑ prizes -- small toys/novelties and wrapped candy assortment

Supplies & Decorations

- ❑ paper products (tablecloth, plates, cups, napkins)
- ❑ plastic spoons, forks
- ❑ balloons/streamers (optional)
- ❑ old blankets or sheets

Crowns

- ❑ light-weight yellow poster board (enough to make one 6"x24" strip for each guest)
- ❑ colored markers
- ❑ stapler
- ❑ glue sticks
- ❑ 3 cardboard trays (the type used to hold four six-packs of soda)
- ❑ glitter in shaker jars or roll-on glitter
- ❑ sequins and spangles, glittery confetti
- ❑ bits of ribbon, feathers,
- ❑ pom pons and colored tissue paper
- ❑ stick-on gemstones earrings
- ❑ gummed paper stickers, foil star stickers

> *TIP: Catalogs and Arts & Crafts stores are great places to find most of these items.*

Necklaces

- ❑ elastic cord or lanyard
- ❑ wagon wheel pasta
- ❑ rigatoni pasta
- ❑ food coloring or Liquid Watercolor
- ❑ rubbing alcohol
- ❑ reclosable gallon size storage bags
- ❑ plastic tracing figures--tropical, circus, zoo, dinosaur (or shapes cut out of construction paper)
- ❑ assortment of items with large holes for easy stringing (optional)
- ❑ hole punch
- ❑ scissors
- ❑ 3 cardboard cartons/trays (the type that hold four six-packs of canned soda)

Get-Together Time

- ❑ 1 hand mirror
- ❑ 4-8 small items related to the theme: costume jewelry (earrings, necklace, ring, bracelet, etc.), mirror, shiny stones or a rock sprayed gold, a small bag of glitter (fairy dust), etc.
- ❑ scarf/cloth napkin or bandanna
- ❑ plastic bracelets and rings (1 for each guest)

Games & Activities

- ❑ Purchase 1 wand for each guest or make with 12" sticks, yellow poster board stars, and crepe paper or ribbon
- ❑ CD/tape player
- ❑ Music -- fast and slow selections, also marching music. Suggestions: Disney's The Lion King and Aladdin soundtracks.
- ❑ bag of chocolate candy gold foil coins or 1 rock sprayed gold

Refreshments

- ❏ make or purchase a cake
- ❏ candles and matches
- ❏ ice cream
- ❏ muffin or cupcake paper liners and muffin tin
- ❏ liter bottles of Cherry 7-Up
- ❏ large plastic trash bag

Present Opening

- ❏ 1 star wand (made or purchased)
- ❏ CD/tape player
- ❏ music --Disney's "*When You Wish Upon A Star*" song
- ❏ paper trash bag
- ❏ scissors

Don't Forget

- ❏ camera
- ❏ video camera
- ❏ film
- ❏ 1-2 helpers
- ❏ back-up batteries for CD/tape player and camera

Get Set!

The Day Before the Party:

❑ Make the cake (if that was your child's choice).

❑ Scoop the ice cream into cupcake liners placed in muffin tin. Store in the freezer.

❑ Cut yellow poster board for crowns into 6"x24" pieces; cut a zigzag pattern along one of the long sides.

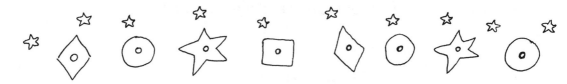

❑ Cut the colored construction paper into shapes (stars, hearts, moons, etc.) Use small cookie cutters as patterns. Punch a hole in the middle of each shape for stringing.

❑ Color wagon wheel and rigatoni pasta according to the recipe which follows.

❑ Cut elastic cord or lanyard into 36" pieces and tie a piece of wagon wheel pasta onto one end of each piece.

COLORED MACARONI RECIPE

Ingredients

rubbing alcohol
several colors of food coloring or Liquid Watercolor
Uncooked wagon wheel or rigatoni pasta
newspaper
reclosable gallon size plastic bags

Instructions (for each color):

1. Put ½ cup rubbing alcohol into a reclosable, gallon size plastic storage bag.

2. Add several drops of food coloring or a big squirt of Liquid Watercolor. Add more coloring if you'd like a brighter, darker color.

3. Place a handful of uncooked wagon wheel and rigatoni pasta in the bag. Seal the bag.

4. Leave the pasta in the bag until it turns the desired color. Turn the bag over or shake it every once in awhile so all the pasta gets colored.

5. Dry pasta on newspaper. Throw away the bags you used to color the pasta.

6. Store colored pasta in empty reclosable gallon size storage bags.

❏ Make the magic wands if you decided not to buy them:

Instructions for Making Magic Wands

1. Collect sticks or roll three sheets of newspaper together widthwise and tape them together for each wand.

2. Wrap each stick or newspaper roll in aluminum foil, and secure with tape.

3. Cut out star shapes from yellow poster board.

4. Decorate with glitter (optional).

5. Cut long strips of ribbon or crepe paper for streamers.

6. Glue or tape star and streamers to the top of the wand.

The Day of the Party:

❑ Decorate the party area (optional).

❑ Pick up the birthday cake if you ordered one.

❑ Fill the cooler, box or container with the small toys and assorted wrapped candies you bought for prizes. Stir them up...now you have a treasure chest!

❑ Spread out blankets or sheets for the Make 'n Create areas. Place materials for the areas in cardboard trays on the blankets.

  * Party Bags
  * Crowns
  * Necklaces

❑ Clear an area to use later for Get-Together time and present opening.

❑ Don't forget to spruce up the yard as needed (especially if you have pets!)

❑ Clear space to dance, march and run.

❑ Set the table or decide where you'll put the tablecloth on the ground for serving refreshments.

Let's Party!

Make 'n Create

Station helpers at the Make 'n Create areas. When guests arrive, send them to the Party Bag area. *After guests finish each project, direct them to the treasure chest to pick a prize and a piece of candy and put them in their party bags.* Place the party bag behind the treasure chest, then send them to the next Make 'n Create area. Keep the tempo fast and fun!

Party Bags

1. Give each guest a flat white lunch bag.
2. Helper or guest writes guest's name on the front of the bag.
3. Guest decorates the bag.

Crowns

1. Helper or guest writes guest's name on the crown.
2. Guest uses the glue stick, markers and art materials to decorate the crown.
3. Helper staples the crown together so it fits around the guest's head.
4. Encourage guests to wear crowns during the party.

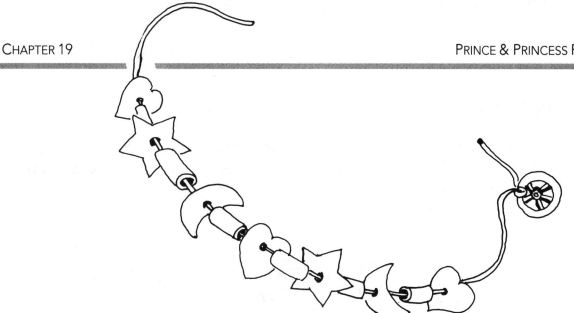

Necklaces

1. Give each guest a piece of cord or lanyard for stringing with colored pasta and precut paper shapes or plastic tracing figures.

2. Encourage the kids to be creative. Suggest alternating pasta and paper shapes. Discourage them from stringing just paper shapes or plastic figures; the pasta helps separate the shapes or figures.

3. Tie the ends together and cut off the excess cord.

4. Guest wears the necklace or puts it into party bag.

Get-Together Time

Spread out a blanket or sheet and ask the guests to sit around the edge in a circle. (While you're doing this, a helper can hide rings and bracelets in an area not visible to the guests). Lead the kids in the "Mirror, Mirror" game to recognize everyone who came to the party.

Mirror, Mirror

☛ Ask the guests to recall the scene from the story *Snow White* in which the mirror is asked, "Mirror, mirror on the wall who's the fairest one of all?"

☛ Tell them to pass the hand mirror from guest to guest as everyone chants, "Mirror, mirror on the wall who's the fairest one of all?"

☛ Whoever is holding the mirror at the end of the question says his or her name.

☛ If the mirror happens to end up with someone who's already had a turn, he or she gives it to a person on either side who hasn't had a turn.

☛ Have fun -- try having the guests repeat the question very quickly or in slow motion.

☛ Continue the game until everyone, including you, has said his or her name.

Hidden Jewels

Still sitting in a circle, show guests the theme-related items (jewelry, etc...the number should equal the birthday child's age) you gathered together ahead of time. Place them on the ground in front of you and name each item.

1. Cover the items with the magic scarf (napkin or bandanna).

2. Instruct guests to say the magic words, "*Bippity, Boppity, Boo!*" while they wave one hand in front of them.

3. Conceal one item as you lift off the scarf and ask guests, "What's missing?"

4. Call on a guest to name the missing item. After the guest has named it, return the item to its original spot.

5. Continue the game using stronger magic by waving 2 hands over the scarf and repeating the magic words.

6. Conceal two items as you lift off the scarf. Ask two different guests to each name one of the missing items.

7. On the final round, shake both hands over the scarf (for really powerful magic!) while saying the magic words.

8. Conceal all the items as you lift off the scarf. Ask the guests who haven't had a turn yet to name the missing items.

Ring & Bracelet Hunt

✳ While the guests are still sitting in a circle, show them a ring and a bracelet like the ones your helper has hidden.

✳ Instruct them to each find one ring and one bracelet and show them to a helper.

✳ Have the birthday child lead the guests to the hunt area.

✳ When the guest shows the ring and bracelet to the helper, direct them to the treasure chest to pick another prize and piece of candy, then put everything -- bracelet, ring, prize and candy, in the party bag -- and put it behind the treasure chest again.

Games & Activities

Intersperse these games before and after refreshments or present opening. Make sure you do at least one or two before sitting down to eat.

Magic Wand Dancing

1. Give each guest a magic wand. Instruct guests to start dancing, magic wand in hand, when the music starts and freeze when the music stops.

2. After they've danced awhile, challenge them to dance in their:

    ❧ *high space* (dancing on their tiptoes with magic wands above their heads).
    ❧ *low space* (squatting down with their magic wands low to ground).
    ❧ *middle space* (waving their magic wands back and forth at waist level).

3. Try to trick the guests by starting and stopping the music quickly. Kids love surprise.

4. Don't forget to change the tempo by alternating slow and fast music and suggesting the children twirl, leap, and float to the music.

Royal Parade

1. With magic wands still in hand, line guests up behind the birthday child.

2. Instruct guests to start marching when the music starts and stop when it stops.

3. Allow the birthday child to lead the parade where she or he pleases.

4. Play some rousing music like "*I Just Can't Wait To Be King*" from Disney's *Lion King.*

5. The parade's over when the song ends.

6. Ask the children to place their wands in their party bags.

Lost Gold

Guests sit in a circle around a sheet or blanket. Show them the precious gold (the bag of chocolate gold coins or the gold rock). Tell them the precious gold will be lost.

1. Have the birthday child leave the room while you give the gold to a guest. The guest hides the gold underneath his or her legs.

2. Tell the birthday child to come back and find the missing gold.

3. The birthday child walks around inside the circle.

4. Everyone sitting in the circle begins clapping. They clap slower and more softly when the birthday child moves away from the gold and louder and faster when the birthday child gets closer to the gold.

5. Guests clap their loudest and fastest when the birthday child stands directly in front of the guest who is hiding the precious gold.

6. The birthday child points to the guests he or she thinks is hiding the gold. If the guess is incorrect, the birthday child continues walking and listening until he or she guesses correctly.

7. When the birthday child guesses who has the gold, that person gives the birthday child the gold and leaves the room.

8. The birthday child gives the gold to another guest who hides it beneath his or her legs.

9. The birthday child joins the circle of kids sitting on the floor.

10. Continue the game until everyone's had a turn finding the gold.

Knights & Dragons

1. Set two boundaries at either end of an empty space outdoors.

2. Designate a guest to be the dragon and stand in the middle of the empty space.

3. The other guests are the knights and stand behind one of the boundaries.

4. The dragon says, "All knights run!" and the knights run toward the opposite boundary.

5. The dragon tries to touch as many knights as possible.

6. If the dragon touches a knight, that knight becomes a dragon too and tries to touch the knights as they run between the boundaries.

7. Each time the dragons say, "All knights run!" the knights run to the opposite boundary.

8. Continue the game until all the knights have been touched and turned into dragons. The last child to be touched becomes the new dragon and starts the next game of Knights & Dragons.

Let's Eat

Refer to the *"High Drama~Serving the Cake"* section in the LET'S PARTY! chapter for the basics.

Open Presents

When You Wish Upon a Star

Follow the guidelines in the *"Opening Presents~The Center of Attention!"* section of the LET'S PARTY! chapter with these variations: play *When You Wish Upon a Star* and pass around a magic wand.

The Party's Over!

The guests visit the treasure chest one more time to pick out a last prize and candy. Send the guests home with party bags, crowns, necklaces and magic wands. Have the birthday child stand at the doorway and thank each guest individually for coming to the royal bash.

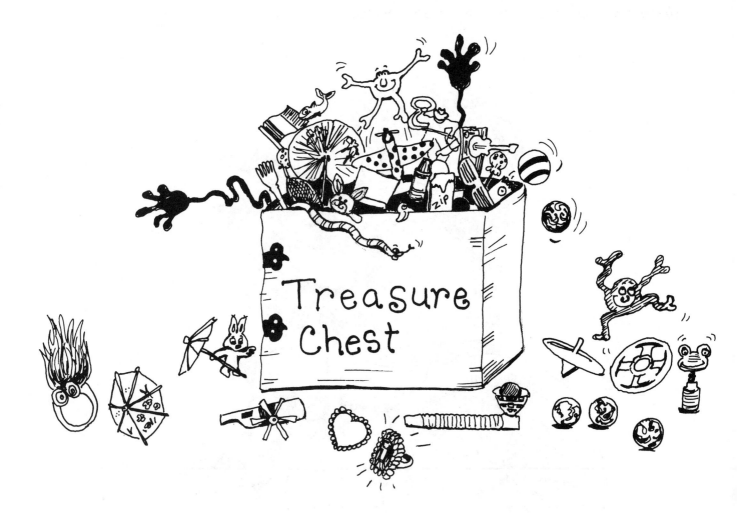

TEDDY BEAR PICNIC PARTY

For every bear that ever there was
Will gather there for certain because...
Today's the day the teddy bears have their picnic!

Bears, bears everywhere! Decorate the yard and party area with them and invite guests to bring their favorite bear or stuffed animal to the party. Almost every child has a most loved or special stuffed friend, so why not have a party that includes them?!! Take a look at all the things the guests and bears will do...

Teddy Bear Picnic Party Snapshot

AGES:	4 TO 8 YEARS
TOTAL TIME:	1-1/2 TO 2 HOURS

10 minutes	**Greet Guests** Teddy Bear Awards
20 minutes	**Make 'n Create** Party Bags Teddy Bear Puppets
15 to 20 minutes	**Get-Together Time** Bear Introductions Teddy Bear Turn Around Rainbow Bear Hunt
15 to 20 minutes	**Games & Activities** Teddy Bear Parade Gummy Bear Relay Going On A Bear Hunt
20 to 30 minutes	**Let's Eat!** Teddy Bear Cupcakes Teddy Bear Cookies Teddy Bear Tea
15 to 20 minutes	**Open Presents** Musical Bears

Get Ready!

Invitations

Ask each guest to bring a favorite bear or stuffed toy animal.

Checklists

Supplies & Decorations

- ❏ paper products (tablecloth, plates, cups, napkins)
- ❏ plastic spoons
- ❏ balloons/streamers (optional)
- ❏ old blankets, sheets or plastic tablecloths to put on the ground for each Make 'n Create area and for serving refreshments
- ❏ 3-4 extra teddy bears to loan to children who've forgotten theirs

Party Bags

- ❏ white paper lunch bags
- ❏ watercolor markers/crayons
- ❏ teddy bear stickers and/or rubber stamps
- ❏ rubber stamp ink pads (washable/child safe)
- ❏ prize chest (small cooler, box or container)
- ❏ prizes -- bear toys and small novelties (erasers, pencils, pencil tops, jewelry, stationery, note pads, stickers, etc.)

Teddy Bear Awards

- ❏ red construction paper
- ❏ 2" gold foil notary seals (available at stationery/office supply store)
- ❏ ribbon (½" to 1" wide)
- ❏ scotch tape
- ❏ hole punch
- ❏ safety pins
- ❏ fine point black permanent marker
- ❏ scissors
- ❏ gummed or self-adhesive hole reinforcements

Teddy Bear Puppets

- ❏ brown paper lunch-size bags or smaller
- ❏ pink construction paper
- ❏ colored markers/crayons
- ❏ glue sticks

Get-Together Time

- ❏ Brach's individually wrapped Rainbow Bear jelly candy found in bulk candy bins at grocery stores. Buy enough (plus extra) so each guest can find as many candies as the birthday child is years old.

Games & Activities

- ❏ CD/tape player
- ❏ plastic spoons (one for each guest)
- ❏ *"Teddy Bears' Picnic"* song from the Teddy Bears' Picnic book with audio cassette by Jim Kennedy or *"There's A Hippo In My Bathtub"* by Anne Murray
- ❏ one pound Gummy Bear candy
- ❏ 1-2 plastic bear-shaped honey containers (find at grocery store)

Refreshments

- ❏ cupcakes and frosting --make or purchase as the birthday child chooses
- ❏ candy to decorate the cupcake -- M&M's, jelly beans, red shoestring licorice, chocolate sprinkles, Lifesaver Gummie Savers, etc.
- ❏ teddy bear-shaped cookies or graham crackers
- ❏ 1 small jar Tang
- ❏ ½ cup instant tea
- ❏ powdered cinnamon
- ❏ powdered cloves
- ❏ sugar
- ❏ 1 large envelope powdered lemonade
- ❏ jug of water
- ❏ 2-4 toy tea sets (easy to borrow --just ask friends)
- ❏ large plastic trash bag

Present Opening

- ❏ teddy bear (one belonging to and chosen by the birthday child)
- ❏ *"Teddy Bear's Picnic"* music
- ❏ CD/tape player
- ❏ paper trash bag
- ❏ scissors

Don't Forget

- ❏ candles and matches
- ❏ camera
- ❏ video camera
- ❏ film
- ❏ 1 or 2 helpers (spouse, older siblings, relatives, babysitters, friends)
- ❏ portable CD/tape player
- ❏ back-up batteries for CD/tape player and camera

Get Set!

The Day Before the Party

☐ Make and frost cupcakes (if that was the birthday child's choice).

☐ Make Teddy Bear Awards:

  ☐ Cut red construction paper into 2-½" circles (a little bit larger than the gold notary seals).

  ☐ Stick gold seals to red construction paper circles.

  ☐ Attach two 3" pieces of ribbon to the back of each red circle with scotch tape.

  ☐ Punch a hole at the top of the award (through the red paper and the gold seal.)

  ☐ Adhere gummed or self-adhesive hole reinforcements to both sides of the punched hole.

  ☐ Put a safety pin through the hole.

❑ Empty plastic bear(s) of honey and wash them out.

❑ Prepare material for Teddy Bear Puppets.

    ❑ Cut out arms, ears and tummies from pink construction paper. Remember, they'll need to fit on the lunch bag.

❑ Make instant Teddy Bear Tea mixture as follows:

TEDDY BEAR TEA RECIPE

INGREDIENTS

1 small jar Tang
½ cup instant tea
1 tsp. cinnamon
½ tsp. cloves
½ cup sugar
1 large envelope powdered lemonade

INSTRUCTIONS

1. Combine all ingredients and mix well.

2. Store in an airtight container.

3. For children's tea: add I tsp. to cup of cold water. Stir well.

4. For adult's tea: add 2 tsp. to cup of boiling water. Stir well.

The Day of the Party

❑ Decorate the party area (optional).

❑ Pick up cupcakes if you ordered them.

❑ Fill the prize chest with toy assortment -- stir it up.

❑ Place Teddy Bear Awards and a permanent marker near the entrance.

❑ Set up the following Make 'n Create areas. Spread out sheets or blankets. Place materials on top of them.

♥ Party Bag making area

♥ Teddy Bear Award area

♥ Teddy Bear Puppet making area

❑ Decide where you'll hold the Get-Together Time and Present Opening. Clear enough space to spread a blanket out for everyone to sit around.

❑ Clear the yard for games and activities. (Be sure to clean up after pets!) You'll need enough space for the parade and relay races.

❑ Decide where you'll serve refreshments (a table or a place to spread a tablecloth out on the ground (Don't forget the tea sets.)

❑ Put out a jug of ice water with small paper cups.

Let's Party!

Greet Guests

Teddy Bear Awards

1. As each guest arrives, ask for the bear's name or what the guest calls the bear (e.g., "Huggy Bear," "Purple Bear," "Dancing Bear," etc.)

2. If the guest doesn't have a name for the bear, help make one up. (You might suggest one that relates to the bear's features, e.g., -- "Furry Bear," or "Soft Bear.")

3. Write the bear's name on the gold foil seal with the permanent marker and pin this *Teddy Bear Award* on the bear.

4. Place the bear, sitting up, in a designated area.

Make 'n Create

Direct guests to the Make 'n Create areas. *After finishing each area, have them go to the prize chest, select a prize and piece of candy and put them in their party bags. Set their party bags behind the prize chest and send them to the next area.*

Party Bags

1. Give each guest a flat white lunch bag.
2. Helper or guest writes guest's name on the front of the bag.
3. Guest decorates the bag.

Teddy Bear Puppets

1. Give each guest a small brown paper bag and show them where to draw the puppet's eyes, nose and mouth on the bottom flap. Make a sample puppet to demonstrate but don't do it for the guests.

2. Guests glue on ears, arm, and tummy.

3. When everyone's finished, show the kids how to put their hands inside the bag to move the puppets' mouths.

4. Suggest the guests play with their puppets and together put on a puppet show.

Get-Together Time

Spread out a blanket or sheet and have all children sit with their bears in a circle around the edge of it. Have a helper hide the Rainbow Bear jelly candy (for the Rainbow Bear Hunt) in an area of the yard not visible to the guests.

Bear Introductions

1. Introduce the birthday child first.

2. Ask the birthday child to introduce his or her bear.

3. Ask a few questions about the birthday child's bear then read the Teddy Bear Award.

4. Continue around the circle, introducing each guest and asking the guest to introduce his or her bear.

5. Encourage participation by asking questions such as:

    * "What's the bear's name?"
    * "Was it a gift?"
    * "How long has your bear lived with you?"
    * "Do you sleep with your bear?"

6. Again, read the Teddy Bear Award before continuing on to the next guest.

Teddy Bear Turnaround

While still in a circle, have the guests stand up with bears in hand. Ask them to chant this rhyme with you as they and their bears perform the actions in the song. Repeat the rhyme at least once or twice. Children learn from repetition.

Teddy bear, teddy bear, turn around.
(hold bear and turn around in a circle)

Teddy bear, teddy bear, touch the ground.
(lower teddy bear's arms to the ground))

Teddy bear, teddy bear, jump up high.
(hold bear and jump in place)

Teddy bear, teddy bear, touch the sky.
(lift the bear high into the air)

Teddy bear, teddy bear touch your nose.
(move bear's arm to touch bear's nose)

Teddy bear, teddy bear, touch your toes.
(lower bear's arms to touch bear's toes)

Teddy bear, teddy bear, turn out the light.
(move bear's arm in flicking motion while clicking your tongue)

Teddy bear, teddy bear, say good night.
(rock bear in arms while you make snoring sounds)

Rainbow Bear Hunt

1. Have guests retrieve their party bags from behind the prize chest and return to the Get-Together Time circle.

2. Show guests a sampling of the individually wrapped Rainbow Bear jelly candies that are hidden in a special area for the Rainbow Bear Hunt.

3. Instruct guests to find as many bear candies as the birthday child is old (e.g., J. P. Is six years old, so every guest finds six candies). Demonstrate by counting out six Rainbow Bear jelly candies.

4. Have the birthday child lead the guests to the Rainbow Bear Hunt area.

5. Instruct the guests to put the candies they find in their party bags and show them to an adult or helper. Have extras on hand for those who find only a few.

Games & Activities

Teddy Bear Parade

Guests retrieve bears and line up behind the birthday child. Birthday child, with
bear in hand, leads the parade marching to the music *"Teddy Bears' Picnic."*
Parade starts when the music begins and stops when the music ends.

Gummy Bear Relay

Cooperation is a natural with this game as children must all work together to feed the hungry bear. There's no waiting in line either.

1. Place an empty plastic bear bottle(s) on a flat surface at one end of the party area. Place a bowl of Gummy Bear candy at the other end.

2. Tell the guests the empty bear(s) is hungry and they're going to feed him his favorite food--Gummy Bears! Give each guest a plastic spoon.

3. At the signal "GO," each child scoops a Gummy Bear onto his or her spoon. The kids may need to use their fingers. That's okay. These critters are sticky!

4. Kids walk to the empty bear at the other end of the party area, balancing the Gummy Bear in the spoon, then drop the candy into the hungry bear's belly.

5. Kids return to the bowl to get another Gummy Bear and repeat the process

6. Continue the game until the bear(s) is full.

If children ask to do it again, empty the bear(s) and start over with hungry bears. When the game is over, ask the children to get their party bags and distribute the remaining untouched Gummy Bears equally among them. Try this variation for older children: hold the spoons in their mouths while walking to and from the hungry bear.

Going On a Bear Hunt

Have guests sit around the edge of a blanket as they did earlier at Get-Together Time. Ask them to echo everything you say and pantomime all the actions following your lead.

Begin by slapping one thigh then the other with your hands to a regular beat (to make the sounds of a person walking) and say:

"We're going on a bear hunt!"
(children repeat)

And we're not afraid.
(children repeat)

All right, let's go
(keep slapping thighs alternately)

Looking for a bear
(children continue to echo each line as the hunt continues)

Oh look!
There's a great big bridge.
Can't go around it.
Can't go under it.
Gotta walk over it.
(pound chest with alternating fists)

Oh look!
I see a field of tall grass.
Can't go around it.
Can't go under it.
Gotta walk through it.
(rub palms of hands together in a swishing motion)

Oh look!
I see a lake.
Can't go around it.
Can't go under it.
Gotta swim across it.
(make swimming motions with arms)

Oh look!
There's a tall tree.
Can't go around it.
Can't go under it.
Gotta climb up it.
(move arms in climbing motion. When you reach the top, hold your hand over your
eyes to shade them and say...)

Oh look!
I see a cave.
Let's go down and see what's inside.
(put your arms around the "tree" and slide down. When you reach the bottom, slap
your thighs slowly and softly as you walk to the cave)

Ooh -- It's cold in here.
Ooh --It's dark in here.
I can't see anything.
But...
I feel something warm...
I feel something furry...
It's a bear!!! Run!!!
(slap your thighs in a fast pace as if running and repeat motions in reverse order very
quickly saying...)

Climb up the tree.
Swim across the lake.
Through the grass.
Over the bridge.

Whewwwww, we're safe!

We went on a bear hunt!
(children repeat)

And we weren't afraid!
(children repeat)

Let's Eat!

Set the table (or the tablecloth on the ground) with tea sets, spoons, cups, saucers, teapots of water, sugar bowls filled with instant Teddy Bear Tea mix, plates of teddy bear-shaped cookies or graham crackers, etc.

Guests sit next to their bears. Pass out frosted cupcakes and instruct the guests to make bear faces on their cupcakes with candy: M&M's or jelly beans for eyes and nose, red shoestring licorice for mouth, Lifesaver Gummie Savers for ears and chocolate sprinkles for fur.

When the guests have finished decorating their cupcakes, let the birthday child put candles on his or her cupcake and proceed with the basics as outlined in the *"High Drama~Serving the Cake"* section in the LET'S PARTY chapter.

Open Presents

Refer to the basic instructions in the *"Opening Presents~The Center of Attention!"* section of the LET'S PARTY! chapter.

Musical Bears

- ❧ Have guests retrieve their presents and sit in a circle as they did earlier for Get-Together Time.

- ❧ Instruct the guests to put their presents behind their backs.

- ❧ Seat the birthday child in the middle of the circle.

- ❧ Pass around the birthday child's teddy bear or other toy chosen by the birthday child while playing *"Teddy's Bear Picnic."*

- ❧ When the music stops, the guest who is holding the bear gives the present behind his back to the birthday child.

- ❧ The guest continues to hold the bear until the birthday child has opened the present and "Thank you" and "You're welcome" have been exchanged.

- ❧ The music starts again and guests continue to pass the bear.

- ❧ The game ends when all the guests have given their gifts.

The Party's Over

Distribute any left over Teddy Bear cookies or graham crackers evenly among the party bags. Have the guests visit the prize chest one more time and pick out another prize or, if there are enough prizes left, as many prizes as the birthday child is years old.

Gather Teddy Bear Puppets and send them home with the guests. Don't forget to send home their personal bears complete with Teddy Bear Awards!

The birthday child stands by the door to thank guests "beary" much for coming to the Teddy Bear Picnic Party.

SILLY SLIMY YUCKY MUCKY PARTY

Let your birthday child make a mess and have the time of his or her life. Guests will love it as they go up to their elbows in Flubber and Clean Mud! You can actually make these "tactiley" pleasing concoctions right in your own kitchen. You'll find the materials on your grocery or craft store shelf -- and they're inexpensive!! Let guests make their own single portion recipes or make it in bulk and send your guests home with bags of the stuff.

Have Fun and Get Slimed!

There's more too, if you choose: painting with worms (rubber, that is)! Let kids make their own Floppy Flippers and play Floppy Flipper Wimbledon. Or, how about taking those paper wads and having a Snowball Throw? What are you waiting for? Choose your child's favorites -- have FUN -- and get SLIMED!

Warning: Don't try to do *all* these recipes and activities!! You'll never surface from under the globs of gunk. This party can be done year after year by trying different recipes or repeating favorites. Kids of all ages never get enough of it! Many adults enjoy this party as much (maybe more than!) their kids.

Silly Slimy Yucky Mucky Party Snapshot

AGES: **4 TO 12**
TOTAL TIME: **1-1/2 TO 2 HOURS**

30 minutes   **Make 'n Create**
                       (Choose 2-3)

                       Party Bags
                       Flubber Fun
                       Wacky Wubber
                       Goop
                       Clean Mud
                       Worm Painting
                       Floppy Flippers

15-20 minutes   **Get-Together Time**
                       Worm Squirm
                       Don't Bug Me
                       Spider Ring Hunt

20-30 minutes   **Games & Activities**
                       Scrambled Eggs & Icebergs
                       Floppy Flipper Wimbeldon
                       Snowball Throw
                       Tails

15-20 minutes   **Let's Eat!**
                       Dirt Cups
                       Beetle Juice

15-20 minutes   **Open Presents**
                       Itsy Bitsy Spider

Get Ready!

Invitations

Request that guests wear clothes they can get dirty in!

Checklists:

Supplies & Decorations

- ❏ tablecloth and napkins
- ❏ clear plastic cups, spoons
- ❏ balloons/streamers (optional)
- ❏ old blankets or sheets and plastic tablecloths (I buy a roll of plastic from a party supply store)
- ❏ buckets of water
- ❏ bunches of rags
- ❏ paper towels

Party Bags

- ❏ white paper lunch bags
- ❏ watercolor markers/crayons
- ❏ stickers (bugs, worms, etc.)
- ❏ rubber stamps to go with theme, ink pads (washable/child safe)

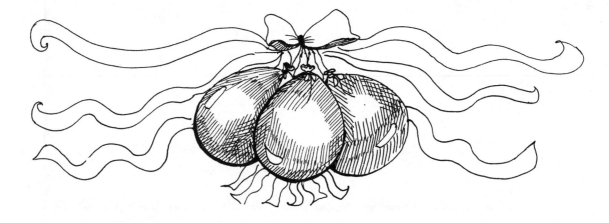

Flubber Fun

- ❏ 2 cups Elmer's Glue-All
- ❏ powdered borax
- ❏ water
- ❏ large bowl
- ❏ measuring cups and spoons
- ❏ clear plastic cups (7 or 9 ounce size) --1 for each guest
- ❏ plastic spoons --1 for each guest
- ❏ 9" plastic plates -- 1 for each guest
- ❏ 1 box plastic straws (non-bendable)
- ❏ reclosable quart size storage bags
- ❏ food coloring, Liquid Watercolor or liquid tempera paint (optional)
- ❏ permanent marker

Wacky Wubber

- ❏ Elmer's Glue-All
- ❏ liquid starch
- ❏ measuring spoons
- ❏ clear plastic cups (7 or 9 ounce size) -- 1 for each guest
- ❏ plastic spoons -- 1 for each guest
- ❏ food coloring , Liquid Watercolor or liquid tempera paint (optional)
- ❏ plastic eggs -- 1 for each guest
- ❏ 9" plastic plates -- 1 for each guest
- ❏ permanent marker

Goop

- ❏ 1 box cornstarch
- ❏ water
- ❏ measuring spoons
- ❏ food color, Liquid Watercolor, liquid tempera paint (optional)
- ❏ 7 or 9 ounce clear plastic cups --1 for each guest
- ❏ 9" plastic plates --1 for each guest
- ❏ plastic spoons --1 for each guest

Clean Mud

- ❏ 3 rolls toilet paper
- ❏ water
- ❏ 1 small bar Ivory Soap
- ❏ powdered borax
- ❏ large plastic container with lid (e.g., a Rubbermaid storage container)
- ❏ reclosable quart size storage bags
- ❏ permanent marker

Worm Painting

- ❏ vinyl or rubber worms and swivel hooks or safety pins (try sporting goods stores)
- ❏ string or twine
- ❏ 3-4 balloon sticks or bamboo garden sticks (nursery/garden store)
- ❏ paper: typing, computer, art, butcher or shelf paper
- ❏ liquid tempera paint
- ❏ cookie sheets, shallow pans or Styrofoam grocery trays
- ❏ permanent marker

Floppy Flippers

- ❏ paint sticks --1 for each child
- ❏ thin, uncoated 9" paper plates
- ❏ clear packaging tape
- ❏ watercolor markers or crayons
- ❏ assorted stickers
- ❏ rubber stamps to go with theme and ink pads (washable/child safe)
- ❏ stapler

Get-Together Time

- ❏ 1 rubber or vinyl worm
- ❏ 4-10 large plastic or vinyl insects, bugs and creepy crawlers -- e.g., a worm, ant, fly, spider, beetle, snake, bat, centipede, lizard, scorpion, etc.
- ❏ scarf, large cloth napkin or bandanna
- ❏ plastic spider rings (1 for each guest)

Games & Activities

- ❏ 9" or 11" balloons -- 1 for each guest
- ❏ scrap paper (8 ½" x 11") -- 2-3 pieces for each guest
- ❏ a long piece of rope or clothesline
- ❏ wastebasket or brown paper grocery bag
- ❏ 30"-36" piece of mylar, cloth or plastic ribbon or tape for each child
- ❏ CD/tape player
- ❏ music: *"U Can't Touch This"* by Hammer
- ❏ the song, *"The Heat Is On"* by Glenn Frey from the motion picture soundtrack Beverly Hills Cop

Dirt Cup ingredients (see recipe for quantities):

❑ milk

❑ chocolate flavor instant pudding

❑ whipped topping

❑ chocolate sandwich cookies

❑ 7-9 oz. clear plastic cups

❑ Gummy candy worms, frogs, etc.

Beetle Juice ingredients:

❑ ½" - 2" plastic rings or plastic insects (bugs, flies, snakes, ants, etc.)

❑ red fruit punch

❑ ice cube trays

Present Opening

❑ spider -- a puppet or rubber spider or even a spider ring will work -- though a larger size is desirable

❑ CD/tape player

❑ music: "*The Itsy Bitsy Spider*" sung by Little Richard from Disney's For Our Children or by Carly Simon on Coming Around Again

❑ paper trash bag

❑ scissors

Don't Forget...

❑ candles and matches

❑ large plastic trash bag

❑ camera

❑ video camera

❑ film

❑ helpers (spouse, older siblings, relatives, babysitter, teenagers, friends)

❑ portable CD/tape player

❑ back-up batteries for CD/tape player and camera

Get Set!

Four Days Before the Party

❑ Make Clean Mud

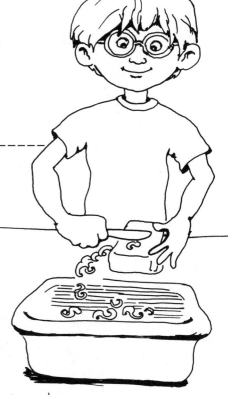

CLEAN MUD RECIPE

INGREDIENTS

3 rolls toilet paper
water
1 small bar Ivory Soap
powdered borax
large plastic container with lid

INSTRUCTIONS

1. Unroll 3 rolls of toilet paper into the large plastic container.

2. Cover with water and let soak for 3 days.

3. After 3 days, drain off water. Don't squeeze!

4. Grate or slice 1 small bar of Ivory Soap into the drained toilet paper.

5. Add 1 ½ cups powdered borax and stir.

6. Cover and let sit overnight.

7. Let kids knead and knead until it looks almost like whipped cream.

Clean Mud is great fun to play in for weeks, even months if it's kept in an airtight container. You may need to add water periodically. You can double the recipe if you use a larger container. Try using colored toilet paper. Kids love it!

Making Clean Mud is half the fun!

The Day Before the Party

❏ make Dirt Cups

DIRT CUP RECIPE

Ingredients

2 cups milk
1 small pkg. chocolate flavor instant pudding
8 oz. tub whipped topping, thawed
16 oz. pkg. chocolate sandwich cookies, crushed
8 plastic cups (7-9 oz.)

Instructions

1. Pour milk into large bowl; add pudding mix. Beat with electric mixer until well blended.

2. Let sit 5 minutes. Stir in whipped topping and ½ the crushed cookies.

3. Place 1 Tbs. of the remaining crushed cookies into each cup.

4. Fill the cups 3/4 full with pudding mixture. Top with more crushed cookies. Refrigerate.

5. Decorate with gummy candy worms, frogs, etc. before serving. Serves 8.

❏ Prepare Beetle Juice: Fill ice cube trays with water. Place one plastic bug or insect ring in each cube of the trays. (If you don't have small toy insects, use jelly or Gummy fruit snacks.) Freeze.

❏ Prepare ingredients for Flubber (this recipe makes enough for 18 single portions--increase if needed):

   * Mix 2 cups of glue and 1 ½ cups water in large bowl. Stir well. Store in an airtight container.

   * Mix 1-1/3 cups hot tap water and 4 tsp. powdered borax until dissolved. Store in an airtight container.

❏ Worm Painting: make 3 or 4 painting poles--attach plastic or vinyl worm to a swivel hook or safety pin, tie a piece of string to the hook or pin, attach the other end of the string to the pole.

❏ Floppy Flippers: tape paint sticks to paper plates for Floppy Flippers. Make one for each guest.

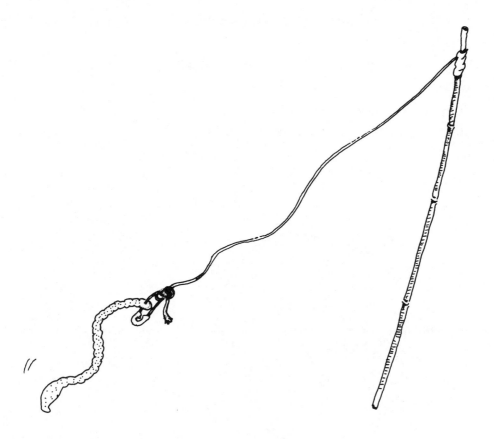

The Day of the Party

❑ Decorate party area (optional).

❑ Spread out plastic sheets or blankets and set out supplies for making:

➤ Party bags

➤ Flubber (glue and powdered borax mixtures)

➤ Wacky Wubber

➤ Goop

➤ Clean Mud

➤ Floppy Flippers

❑ Decide where you'll hold Get-Together and Present Opening. Clear enough space to spread out a blanket or sheet to sit around.

❑ Get the yard ready for games and activities -- make sure you have space for the kids to run and play.

❑ Set up a table for refreshments or decide where you'll put a tablecloth on the ground.

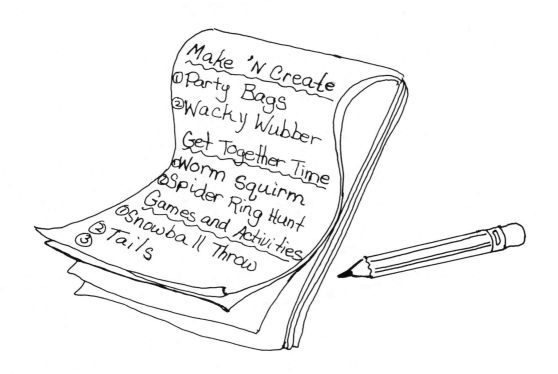

Let's Party!

Station helpers at the Make 'n Create areas. When guests arrive, send them to the Party Bag making area. *After guests finish each project, direct them to the prize chest to pick a prize and a piece of candy and put them in their party bags. Place the party bag behind the prize chest, then send them to the next Make 'n Create area.* Keep the tempo fast and fun!

Make 'n Create

Party Bags

1. Give guests white paper bags.

2. Have the guests write their names on the bags (supply help if needed).

3. Let them decorate the bags to their heart's content.

Flubber Fun

1. Give each guest a clear plastic cup, spoon, straw and plastic plate.

2. Measure 3 Tbs. of the glue solution into the guest's cup.

3. The guest adds 2-3 drops food color, Liquid Watercolor, or liquid tempera paint to his or her glue solution and stirs well. (Optional)

4. The helper adds 1 Tbs. borax solution to each guest's cup.

5. The guest stirs the mixture thoroughly. Suddenly, it becomes thick and slimy and turns into a solid mass. Hey, presto -- Flubber!

6. The guest removes the Flubber from the cup and kneads it until it's smooth. Leave the extra liquid in the cup.

Let the guests play with Flubber on the plastic plates and observe its many properties:

- Hold it up and watch it stretch.
- Roll it into a ball.
- Make it bounce.
- Watch it melt on the plate.
- Wrap Flubber around a straw and blow into it. Blow bubbles so big they pop! Sometimes Flubber makes funny noises when you blow into it. Pardon me!

After they're done experimenting, store each guest's Flubber and straw in a reclosable quart size plastic bag labeled with his or her name. Have the guests put the bags of Flubber in their party bags.

Flubber will eventually grow mold. When it does, throw it away and make some more!

Wacky Wubber

1. Give each guest a clear plastic cup, spoon and plastic plate.

2. Measure 1 Tbs. liquid starch into the cup.

3. Add 2 Tbs. Elmer's Glue-All to the starch.

4. Let it sit for 5 minutes.

5. Guest adds 3 drops food color, Liquid Watercolor, or liquid tempera paint to the mixture. (Optional)

6. Guest stirs mixture in cup until the starch absorbs and color spreads evenly. Tell kids the more they mix the better Wacky Wubber gets!

Use Wacky Wubber like the commercial varieties-- manipulate it, shape it, mold it, bounce it, stretch it, cut it, play, play, play with it! Wacky Wubber will pick up pictures from comics or newspapers after 24 hours.

Store Wacky Wubber in a plastic egg. Write the guest's name on the egg. Have the guests put their eggs in their party bags.

Goop

1. Helper gives guest clear plastic cup (labeled with his or her name), spoon, and plastic plate.

2. Helper measures 2 Tbs. cornstarch into each cup.

3. Guest adds 1 Tbs. water to the cornstarch.

4. If desired, guest adds 2-3 drops food color, Liquid Watercolor or liquid tempera paint.

5. Guest stirs mixture in cup to make Goop.

6. Guest pours Goop onto plate and observes and explores its unique properties.

7. Pick up the Goop and squeeze it -- it's crumbly. Hold it loosely --it oozes through your fingers. You can change Goop from a liquid to a solid by simply squeezing.

8. Try adding more cornstarch-- observe and experiment.

9. Try adding more water --observe and experiment.

10. Helper keeps child's cup of Goop to send home at end of party.

Clean Mud

Clean mud is a unique sensory experience. It feels weird and smells good!

Make Clean Mud available for guests to explore and play with using cups, spoons, and lots of creepy crawlers. Just listen as their imaginations take off!

If they want, put handfuls of the stuff in reclosable quart size storage bags labeled with the guests' names. Have them store it in their party bags.

Worm Painting

1. Set out shallow trays of paint -- at least 2 colors.

2. Place a Worm Painting pole by each tray.

3. Put a piece of paper down on a plastic cloth next to a paint tray.

4. Write the guest's name on the paper.

5. Guest holds fishing pole with worm dangling from it and dunks the worm into a paint tray, making sure the worm is completely covered with paint.

6. Guest then paints by plopping the worm up and down and all around on the piece of paper.

7. To change colors, change poles --leaving the pole used first with its original color.

Tell the guests to look at the design the worms made on the paper. They may see some new colors!

When the guests finish their paintings, send them to the next Make 'n Create area.

Floppy Flippers

1. Give each guest a plain paper plate and ask him or her to decorate it with the available art materials.

2. When the guest is finished, staple the plate to one of the plates which you've taped to a paint stick.

3. Have the guests (or you help) write their names on the paint stick handles.

4. Put the Floppy Flipper aside in a safe place and direct the guest to the next Make 'n Create area.

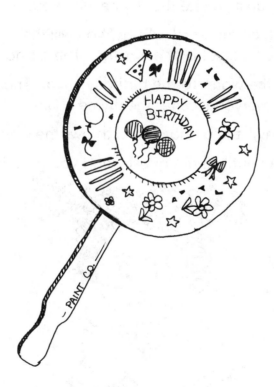

Get-Together Time

Spread out a blanket or sheet and gather the guests into a circle sitting around the edges. Have a helper hide the spider rings in an area of the yard not visible to the guests. Begin with the Worm Squirm Name Game to recognize everyone who's come to the party.

Worm Squirm

1. Present a rubber worm to guests as you recite the following rhyme:

    Hey, Hey
    What do you say?
    Take that worm
    And throw it away!

2. Now have all the guests recite the rhyme with you.

3. Tell the guests that, on the word "_Away_," you will throw the worm. The person who catches the worm says his or her name. There's no need to squirm!

4. Start by throwing the worm to the birthday child. The birthday child says his or her name, then everyone recites the rhyme again.

5. On the word, "Away," the birthday child throws the worm to one of the guests.

6. Continue the game until all the guests, and you too!, have said their names.

Don't Bug Me

Still sitting in a circle, show the children, one at a time, the large rubber bugs, insects and creepy crawlers. Name each one as you put it on the ground in front of you. Put out as many bugs as the birthday child's age plus one more.

1. Cover all the items with the "magic scarf."

2. Instruct the guests to say "magic words" the birthday child has chosen (e.g., "silly, slimy, yucky, mucky" or "ooey, gooey, messamania" or "Hocus Pocus Alamagrossest" or "Don't Bug Me.")

3. Pick up one item, concealed in the scarf, as you lift off the scarf and ask guests, "What's Missing?"

4. Call on a guest to name the missing item.

5. After the guest names the item, return it to its original spot.

6. Continue the game using stronger magic by waving *two* hands over the magic scarf while saying the magic words.

7. This time, remove *two* items as you lift off the scarf. Call on different children to name the missing items.

8. After the guests name the items, return them to their original spots. Cover everything again with the scarf.

9. On the final wave, use the strongest magic of all. Shake *both* hands over the magic scarf while saying the magic words.

10. Remove all the items as you lift off the scarf. Ask guests who haven't had a turn to name the missing items.

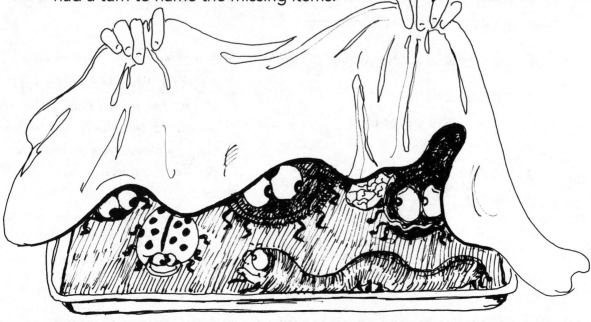

Spider Ring Hunt

While still sitting down, show the guests a spider ring. Instruct them to find one spider ring on their hunt.

Let the birthday child lead the guests to the Spider Ring Hunt area.

The guests may wear their rings or put them in their party bags to take home later.

Games & Activities

Intersperse these games before and after refreshments or present opening. But be sure to do at least one or two before sitting down to eat.

Scrambled Eggs & Icebergs

Have children sit down in game playing area (yard) and listen and watch as you or a helper demonstrate how to play the game. Tell the kids that when they hear...

- "Scrambled eggs," they are to jog around in the open space without bumping into each other.
- "Icebergs," they are to freeze in place without falling down.

Tell them you'll give them other commands too, like "Jump." When they hear the command, they must switch to the new movement. Try to trick them by repeating a command twice in a row!

Hear are some ideas for fun ways to move:

- hop on one foot
- hop on the other foot
- gallop
- tiptoe
- skip

> **PARTY ANIMAL TIP:** Let the birthday child have the power to tell the group which way to move...slow motion, fast forward, sideways, backwards, etc.

Floppy Flipper Wimbledon

Give guests the Floppy Flippers they made.

Have them each pick a balloon, blow it up (or have it blown up) and tie it. Suggest they write their names on the balloons with a permanent marker.

Give the guests time to explore and play with the Floppy Flippers and balloons. Ask them to find out...

- How *high* can they hit their balloons?
- How *far* can they hit them?
- How many times in a row can they hit them? (How about five?!!)
- How *long* can they keep their balloons in the air?
- Can they hit their balloons, *spin around*, then hit them again?

As the kids become more proficient, ask them to try to keep a balloon in the air by hitting it back and forth with a partner. Now they're playing Floppy Flipper Wimbledon!

Suggest they change partners once or twice.

As a further challenge for older kids, have them attempt to keep *two* balloons in the air by themselves or with partners!

REMEMBER: *balloons always require adult supervision!*

Snowball Throw

1. Instruct children to wad up two pieces of 8 ½" x 11" paper into two "snow" balls.

2. Divide the game playing area in half by placing a rope or clothesline on the ground.

3. Divide the guests into equal numbers and place them facing each other on opposite sides of the rope.

4. Have the guests drop their snowballs onto the ground.

5. Tell them to pick up their snowballs (one at a time) and throw them across the rope to the opposite side when the music, "*The Heat Is On,*" starts. (I like to play "*The Heat is On*" because then I can say "throw the snowballs before they melt!" Of course any song will do just fine.)

6. Now we have a good old-fashioned Snowball Throw going on!

7. The Snowball Throw is over when the music ends.

For instant clean-up, suggest the guests try to make a basket as they toss their snowballs into a wastebasket or brown paper grocery bag.

Tails

1. Give each guest a 30" to 36" long tail (cloth, plastic or mylar ribbon or tape).

2. Instruct them to tuck their tails into the back of the waist bands of their pants or skirts.

3. Tell them where to find the Tail Repair Area.

4. When the music starts ("U Can't Touch This"), the guests run around the game playing area and try to pull other children's tails without getting theirs pulled.

5. When they pull off someone's tail, the players drop it on the ground right where they pulled it.

6. Whenever someone's tail gets pulled, he or she goes to the "Tail Repair Area" and puts the tail back on then returns to the game.

7. Note: Guests can pull other guest's tails only if their *own* tails are intact!

8. The game is over when the music ends.

Let's Eat!

Refer to the *"High Drama~Serving the Cake"* section in the LET'S PARTY! chapter for the basics, but substitute Dirt Cups and Beetle Juice (with buggy ice cubes!) for the cake and beverage.

Guests get to eat or keep the bugs in their ice cubes. Watch out for ooey gooey worms in the Dirt Cups!

Open Presents

Follow the basic present opening game instructions in the *"Opening Presents~The Center of Attention!"* section of the LET'S PARTY! chapter but use a stuffed toy spider, puppet spider or spider ring to pass from guest to guest while you play "The Itsy Bitsy Spider" on your tape or CD player. Now you have a new creepy, crawly game: *"Itsy Bitsy Spider!"*

The Party's Over

Make sure the silly slimy yucky mucky stuff the guests made or collected is in their party bags. Don't forget paintings, balloons, Floppy Flippers and Tails.

As guests leave, the birthday child thanks each one individually for sharing in the silly slimy one-of-a-kind birthday party!

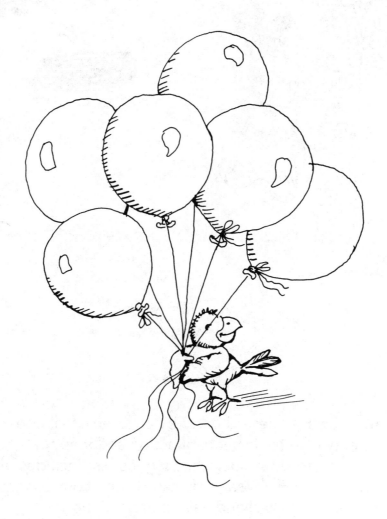

SUPER DARING OBST

This is the Number One requested party by children of all ages. Parents love it too! There are plenty of activities, lots of action and it appeals to both boys and girls. This is *the* party to do if your child's guest list includes all boys and one special girl or vice versa. Five year olds can do the course right along with ten year olds and still feel successful and have barrels of fun.

ACLE COURSE PARTY

TUNNEL ⇨ OF ⇦ NO RETURN

It's easy to find, collect or borrow items to make a simple yet challenging course. Adapt, add and change the course to fit your location and, of course, the birthday child's ideas. If it's hot out, have guests use a spray bottle to hit a target before advancing to the next challenge. You're limited only by your own imagination and creativity. At this party *anything* and *everything* goes!!

Super Daring Obstacle Course Party Snapshot

AGES: **4 TO 12**
TOTAL TIME: **2 HOURS**

30 minutes	**Make 'n Create** Party Bags Froot Loop Necklaces Flubber Fun
15-20 minutes	**Get-Together Time** Koosh Ball Katch Missing Body Parts
20-30 minutes	**Games & Activities** Super Daring Obstacle Course
15-20 minutes	**Let's Eat!** Cake Ice Cream Cold Drinks
20 minutes	**Open Presents** Lucky Dice Roll

Get Ready!

Invitations

Request that guests wear casual play clothes and tennis shoes.

Checklists

Supplies & Decorations

- ❑ paper products (tablecloth, plates, cups, napkins)
- ❑ plastic products (forks, spoons)
- ❑ balloons/streamers (optional)
- ❑ old blankets/sheets or plastic tablecloths

Party Bags

- ❑ white paper lunch bags
- ❑ watercolor markers/crayons
- ❑ sticker assortment (plus alphabet stickers)
- ❑ rubber stamps, stamp pads (washable, non-toxic)
- ❑ small cooler, box or container to use as a prize chest
- ❑ assortment of small novelty toys: puzzles, games, balls, rulers, goofy teeth, plastic animals, insects, tops, whistles, finger puppets, etc. (Let your birthday child choose from the shelves at a party supply store or the pages of a catalog.)
- ❑ selection of individually wrapped candy (lollipops, gum, hard candy, etc.)

Froot Loop Necklaces

- ❏ 2 boxes Froot Loops
- ❏ 1 small box of wagon wheel pasta
- ❏ spool or package of twine or elastic cord (no kite or balloon string)
- ❏ 3 cardboard trays (the kind that hold four 6-packs of soda)

Flubber Fun

- ❏ 2 cups Elmer's Glue-All
- ❏ borax
- ❏ water
- ❏ large bowl
- ❏ half gallon plastic container with lid
- ❏ 3 yogurt containers, small cups or bowls
- ❏ 1 box plastic straws (non-bendable)
- ❏ 1 package 9" plastic plates

Get-Together Time

- ❏ Koosh Ball
- ❏ 5-10 small plastic/rubber body parts (ear, foot, finger, nose, eyeball, toe, heart, lips, teeth, face, etc.) You'll find these at a party supply store or in a catalog.
- ❏ scarf, napkin or bandanna

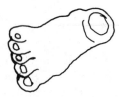

Super Daring Obstacle Course

- ❑ 4 Hula Hoops or bicycle tires
- ❑ piece of rope or clothesline
- ❑ a 2"x4"x8' (or similar size) board to use as a balance beam
- ❑ 4 buckets or small trash cans
- ❑ 2 tennis balls, Nerf balls or bean bags
- ❑ plastic safety cones or chairs (folding, kitchen, patio, children's, etc.)
- ❑ 1 bag of peanuts in the shell
- ❑ 2-3 bags of large marshmallows
- ❑ a cardboard refrigerator box from the appliance store
- ❑ 2 paddle racquets (tennis, badminton, sport, children's, toy or make your own ... See Floppy Flippers in the Silly Slimy Yucky Mucky party section)
- ❑ 10-20 plastic spoons
- ❑ 2 cardboard trays (the kind that hold four six-packs of soda)
- ❑ 2 XL or XXL T-shirts
- ❑ 4 heavy duty plastic trash bags

Refreshments

- ❑ cake --make or purchase according to your child's wishes
- ❑ candles and matches
- ❑ ice cream
- ❑ muffin tin and cupcake paper liners
- ❑ jug or pitcher of lemonade and/or water
- ❑ large plastic trash bag

Present Opening

- ❏ large, over-sized dice (available at party supply stores or through a catalog) or standard size dice
- ❏ wide felt-tipped black marker
- ❏ paper trash bag
- ❏ scissors

Don't Forget

- ❏ camera
- ❏ video camera
- ❏ film
- ❏ 3-4 helpers (spouse, older siblings, relatives, teenagers, friends)
- ❏ portable CD/tape player
- ❏ favorite CD/tapes of birthday child
- ❏ back-up batteries for CD/tape player, camera, video camera

Get Set!

The Day Before the Party

❑ Make the cake (if that was the birthday child's choice)

❑ Scoop ice cream into cupcake liners placed in muffin tin. Put into the freezer.

❑ Cut twine or elastic cord into 36" pieces. Tie a piece of wagon wheel pasta to one end of each piece. If you're using twine, wrap tape around the other end to prevent raveling.

❑   Make Flubber

FLUBBER RECIPE

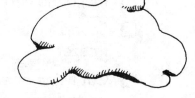

Ingredients

2 cups Elmer's Glue-All
water
borax
food coloring or Liquid Watercolor (optional)

Instructions

1. Mix 2 Cups Elmer's Glue-All with 1-1/2 Cups water in large bowl. (Reduce the water slightly and add food coloring or Liquid Watercolor if you want colored Flubber. Make sure the total liquid equals 1-1/2 Cups.)

2. Pour 1/3 Cup hot tap water into each of three yogurt containers or other small containers. Add 1 tsp. borax to each container and stir until the borax dissolves.

3. Pour the water/borax solution from one of the small containers into the large bowl of glue and water.

4. Stir and gather up the Flubber that forms and sticks to the spoon. Knead the Flubber and place it into a half gallon plastic container with a lid.

5. Repeat the process with the remaining two containers of borax and water.

6. Store the Flubber in the sealed plastic container at room temperature.

Flubber is reusable and will keep at room temperature (no refrigeration needed) for 3-4 weeks. When you see mold, throw it away and make some more! (First try looking at it under a magnifying glass. Hmm. Very interesting.) Flubber will wash off skin and hair (it may take some soaking!) but try to keep the sticky stuff off clothing and carpet.

The Day of the Party

❑ Decorate the party area (optional).

❑ Pick up the cake if you ordered one.

❑ Fill "prize chest" with toy and candy assortment -- stir it up.

❑ Set up the Make 'n Create areas. Spread out blankets, sheets or plastic tablecloths and supplies for:

- Party Bag making area

- Froot Loop Necklace making area (2 cardboard trays filled with Froot Loops, 1 filled with pre-cut necklace strings)

- Flubber Fun area (plastic tablecloth works best for this one.) Set down plastic plates with handfuls of Flubber on them. Set out plastic straws.

❑ Decide where you'll hold the Get-Together Time and Present Opening. Clear the area so all the kids will have space to sit around a blanket or sheet.

❑ Set the table for refreshments or decide on a spot where you can put a tablecloth on the ground.

❑ Set up the Super Daring Obstacle Course. Here are some ideas. Use your imagination to come up with your own variations.

| **Start Line** | Place the rope or clothesline at the beginning of the course. |

Jumping Pattern | Set out bicycle tires or Hula Hoops in a hopscotch pattern (one hoop or tire, then two hoops or tires side by side, then one hoop or tire). Place them so guests must jump over the rope first.

Bridge Walk | Set out two buckets half filled with water at one end of a 2"x4"x8' board laid on the ground.

Ball Toss | Set out balls or bean bags and 2 buckets.

Peanut Maze | Create a maze with traffic safety cones or chairs. Set out peanuts and spoons at the beginning of the maze. Place a cardboard tray at the end of the maze for kids to drop their peanuts and spoons into.

Tunnel Of No Return | Tuck the ends into the cardboard refrigerator box to create a tunnel and place it on the ground.

Trash Bag Shuffle | Place two traffic safety cones or chairs about 8' apart. Place heavy duty plastic trash bags next to the first cone or chair.

T-Shirt Dress & Undress | Put two t-shirts on the ground.

Marshmallow Catch | Place racquets and marshmallows on a chair.

Prize Chest | Place the Prize Chest full of goodies at the end of the course.

Let's Party!

Ask the guests to put their presents in a designated area when they arrive. Prepare for the Lucky Dice Roll present opening game by using a marking pen to write a number on each gift. (The first gift to arrive gets #1, the second gift gets #2, etc.) If there are more than 12 gifts, start the numbering over again after #12.

Direct the guests to the Make 'n Create areas (each staffed with a helper). When they're done at one area, send them to the next until they've completed all three areas. Be sure each guest makes a party bag!!

Make 'n Create

Party Bags

1. Give each guest a flat white lunch bag and instruct them to decorate only the front of it with art materials.

2. Suggest the guests use alphabet stickers to write their name.

3. Provide help with the name if needed. Use stickers or ask the guest what his or her favorite color is. Use that color marker to write the guest's name. Names on bags are a must!

4. When guests are finished, ask them to open up their bags and place them behind the prize chest at the end of the obstacle course.

Froot Loop Necklaces

1. Give the guests pieces of cord or twine and instruct them to string a necklace with Froot Loops.

2. Let the kids eat any Froot Loops that don't have holes in them or are broken.

3. Kids sometimes create patterns with the different colors or even string all the same color.

4. When the guests are finished (they do not have to fill the entire length of the cord), tie the ends together and cut off any excess cord.

5. Guests can wear and eat their edible necklaces or put them in their party bags.

Flubber Fun

Show the guests the many properties of Flubber:

- ✦ Hold it up and watch it stretch. Make sure it lands on the plastic plate or plastic tablecloth. (Once it lands on cement or dirt it's rarely reusable.)

- ✦ Make Flubber into a ball. It's bouncy. Try it!

- ✦ Let Flubber melt on the plate.

- ✦ Blow bubbles with Flubber by wrapping it around a straw and blowing into it. Watch, it really works!! Blow bubbles so big they pop!

Encourage the guests to keep practicing until they get the hang of it. Sometimes Flubber makes funny noises when you blow into it. Excuse me!!

Get-Together Time

Spread out a blanket or sheet and gather guests into a circle sitting around the edge. Begin with the Koosh Ball Katch name game to recognize all the guests who came to your child's birthday party.

Koosh Ball Katch

Show the Koosh Ball to the guests as you recite the following rhyme:

Eeeny Meeny Miny Mo
Catch a Koosh Ball By The Toe
If You Have It Let It Go!

1. Now, have all the guests recite the rhyme with you.

2. Tell the guests they are to throw the Koosh Ball to another guest sitting in the circle on the word "go."

3. The person who catches the Koosh Ball says his or her name.

4. Everyone recites the rhyme again and on the word "go" the person with the Koosh Ball throws it to someone who hasn't had a turn.

5. Koosh Ball Katch ends when everyone has had a turn, including you.

Remember -- the birthday child should be the first one to receive the Koosh Ball!

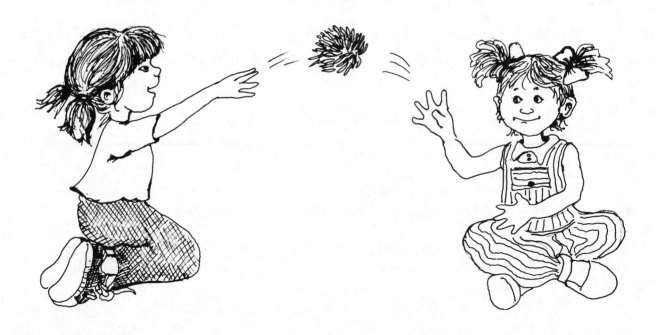

Missing Body Parts

Tell guests they must complete this *mental* challenge before they can proceed with the *physical* challenge of the Super Daring Obstacle Course.

1. Still sitting in a circle, ask guests to identify the plastic body parts you place in front of you. Name each one separately.

2. Put out as many items as the birthday child is old plus one more.

3. Cover all the items with the "magic" scarf or bandanna.

4. Instruct guests to say the "magic words" the birthday child has requested (e.g., "Hocus Pocus Alamagocus," "Abracadabra," etc.) as they wave one hand in front of them.

5. Remove an item, concealing it under the scarf, as you lift off the scarf and ask guests, "What's Missing?"

6. Call on a guest to name the missing body part. After it's been named, return it to its original spot in front of you.

7. Continue the game using stronger magic (waving two hands) over the scarf, saying the magic words and removing two body parts from under the scarf.

8. Ask guests who haven't had a turn to name the missing body parts.

9. On the final wave over the scarf (using the strongest magic of all), shake both hands while saying the magic words and remove all the body parts as you lift off the scarf.

10. Ask guests who haven't had turns to name the missing body parts.

Mental challenge is over when all the body parts have been named.

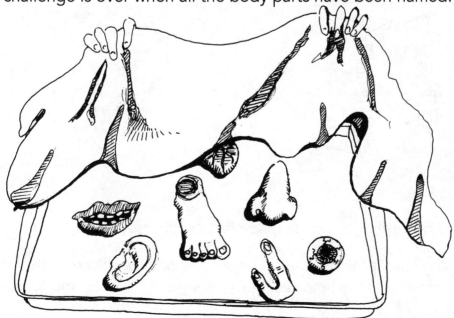

Games & Activities

Preview the Super Daring Obstacle Course!

Tell children they're now ready for the *physical* challenge of the Super Daring Obstacle Course.

Ask them to stand shoulder-to-shoulder on the edge of the course and watch as the birthday child demonstrates the "how-to's" of the course. Guide the birthday child through the course with great fanfare as guests look on. Emphasize the perilous dangers (e.g., "bottomless swamp," and "tunnel of no return.")

At the end of the obstacle course, the birthday child demonstrates catching a marshmallow. Then the birthday child chooses a prize and piece of candy from the prize chest, puts the marshmallow, prize and toy into his or her party bag and places the bag behind the prize chest.

The guests are now ready to line up and start the course.

Play the birthday child's favorite music on the CD or tape player as the guests go through the course as many times as the birthday child is years old (plus more!)

Now Here It Is! The Super Daring Obstacle Course!

Start Line

Jump over the rope or clothesline right into the Jumping Pattern.

Jumping Pattern

Land in the first hoop or tire with two feet, then straddle jump into the hoops or tires placed side by side. End with two feet together again in the last hoop or tire.

Bridge Walk

Walk heel-toe from one end of the board to the other, carrying buckets half filled with water. *Be careful not to fall into the bottomless swamp!*

Ball Toss

Throw the balls or bean bags into the bucket or can. Two can do this at a time.

Peanut Maze

Each guest places a peanut into a plastic spoon and carries it through the maze. Guests put peanuts and spoons in the cardboard tray at the end of the course.

Tunnel Of No Return   Creep through the tunnel on hands and knees (or however you like!)

Trash Bag Shuffle   Put feet into trash bags, pull bags up to waist level, then jump from one chair to the next and back.

T-Shirt Dress & Undress   Kids put t-shirts on and take them off again as quickly as possible.

Marshmallow Catch   An adult or helper uses a paddle, racquet or Floppy Flipper to hit a marshmallow to each guest. The guest catches it.

Prize Chest   The guest chooses one prize and one piece of candy and places them, along with the marshmallow, in his or her party bag. The guest leaves the party bag behind the prize chest and goes on to another circuit of the obstacle course.

Let's Eat!

Refer to the *"High Drama~Serving the Cake"* section in the LET'S PARTY! chapter for the basics.

TIP: Have fun with the "Happy Birthday" song. At Alexander's party, the guests shouted "cha, cha, cha" after each verse!

Open Presents

Lucky Dice Roll

Have guests retrieve the presents they brought and sit around the edges of a sheet or blanket in a circle. Ask them to notice and remember the number written with black marker on their present. They must not tell the birthday child their "lucky" numbers!

1. Tell the guests to put their birthday present behind their backs.

2. The birthday child sits in the middle of the circle with the dice.

3. The birthday child rolls one die or both dice.

4. The guest with that lucky number gives his or her present to the birthday child.

5. If two guests have the same number, (this would happen if you have more than 12 guests), both give their gifts to the birthday child.

6. Continue the game until all the presents have been opened.

7. If a number repeats itself, the birthday child continues to roll, trying to get a number that hasn't shown up yet.

8. You can add to the element of surprise with comments such as, "What lucky number will be next?"

The Party's Over!

Guests collect their party bags from behind the prize chest. Don't forget Froot Loop necklaces. Divide the peanuts used in the *Peanut Maze* into the bags. Send each guest home with some Flubber too. Divide it up and put it into reclosable plastic bags.

As the guests leave, the birthday child thanks each one individually for coming to his birthday party.

CITYWIDE SCAVENGER HUNT PARTY

My all-time favorite party was this bash I threw for my daughter Corrie's twelfth birthday. To this day, she and her friends, now in their twenties, come up to me and say, " that was the best party ever!" I recently duplicated this party for my friend's daughter who was celebrating her twelfth birthday. Her phone is still ringing off the hook with accolades.

Citywide Scavenger Hunt Party Snapshot

AGES: 8 TO 12
TOTAL TIME: 2 TO 2-1/2 HOURS

30 to 40 minutes

Make 'n Create
Crazy Hats
Face Painting and Tattoos

15-20 minutes

Get-Together Time
The Name Game
Memory Challenge
Snicklefritz Partners Switch

40-50 minutes

Games & Activities
Citywide Scavenger Hunt

15-20 minutes

Let's Eat!
Cake
Ice Cream
Beverages

15-20 minutes

Open Presents
Candid Camera

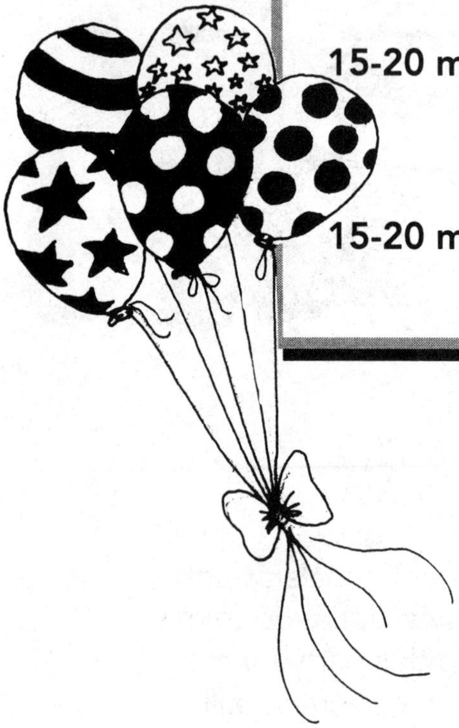

Snickle & Fritz

At this party, mom and dad or two other adults serve as captains of two teams, hereby dubbed Snickle and Fritz, who set off driving through the community to complete a zany list of activities: hug a stranger who's eating pizza, kiss an officer at the local police station etc., etc. Before departing on this wild goose chase, the guests make (and wear!) Crazy Hats out of newspaper and have their faces painted!!

Each antic and activity is recorded with a Polaroid camera. The members of the first team to return receive a rubber chicken. Members of the other team receive a similar gag gift. This is definitely the party to do for the older set. It's a sure-fire crowd pleaser!

Get Ready!

Invitations

Ask guests to wear comfortable clothes that won't mind a little glue, newsprint or paint!

Checklists

Supplies & Decorations

- ❏ paper products (tablecloth, plates, cups, napkins)
- ❏ plastic products (forks, spoons)
- ❏ balloons/streamers (optional)
- ❏ old blankets/sheets or plastic tablecloths

Crazy Hats

- ❏ newspaper -- 3 whole sheets per hat
- ❏ clear, wide packaging tape
- ❏ ribbons, bows (recycle from past present openings)
- ❏ feathers
- ❏ pom pons, buttons
- ❏ sequins, spangles
- ❏ bits of ribbon, color tissue paper, confetti
- ❏ colored glue (buy or make your own with white glue and liquid tempera paint or Liquid Watercolor)
- ❏ glitter in shaker jars
- ❏ shredded tissue, cellophane, Krazy Krinkle paper
- ❏ foam, wood or paper shapes
- ❏ Rainbow Foam Paint and brushes
- ❏ 4 or 5 cardboard cartons or trays (the type used to hold four six-packs of soda)

> **TIP:** Catalogs and Arts & Crafts stores are great places to find most of these.

Face Painting

- ❏ face paints --crayon (Caran D' Ache) or palette (Kryolan) -- water based, washable and non-toxic
- ❏ water
- ❏ paper cups/bowls
- ❏ foam rubber cosmetic sponges
- ❏ cotton swab Q-Tips
- ❏ watercolor-type brushes
- ❏ mirrors
- ❏ facial tissue
- ❏ rubbing alcohol or alcohol towelettes
- ❏ roll-on glitter or fine/superfine glitter
- ❏ tattoos -- removable, washable and non-toxic

Get-Together Time

- ❏ plastic or real banana (not too ripe)
- ❏ 8-12 ordinary items: pencil, scissors, spoon, crayon, coin, small toy, candle, bottle cap, cork, eraser, paper clip, small ball, marker, rubber band, key, toothbrush, cotton ball, etc.
- ❏ tray or cookie sheet
- ❏ a cloth napkin, scarf or bandanna
- ❏ one fancy pencil for each guest
- ❏ one mini notebook for each guest

Games & Activities

- ❏ "Thank You" sheets (20+) to give to people (good-natured and good- humored souls) who helped the teams complete an activity. (These are easy to create and duplicate on a computer or copier.)

THANK YOU!
for being a
GOOD SPORT
&
Making Lindsey's
Birthday Party
FUN!!!!

❏ Copies of the rules and activities
for the Citywide Scavenger Hunt
for each guest

❏ 2 or more cars with enough seat
belts for every guest at the party

❏ 2 Polaroid cameras and at least 4
packages of film (10 pictures per roll).
It's always better to have too much film
than not enough

❏ Adult drivers, wearing watches, for
each car

❏ Two types of gag gifts -- enough for
the members of each team. Favorites
include rubber chickens, hand buzzers,
trick gum, finger traps and corny key
chains. A catalog or party supply store
is a good bet for finding these items.

Refreshments

❏ cake --make or purchase

❏ candles and matches

❏ ice cream

❏ muffin tin and foil bake cups

❏ cooler of canned sodas, waters or juices

❏ large plastic trash bag

Present Opening

❏ scissors

❏ paper grocery bag

Don't forget

❏ more Polaroid film to take those candid shots of the guests in their
Crazy Hats

Get Set!

A Few Days Before the Party

Make up sheets of Rules and Activities for the Citywide Scavenger Hunt. Of course, make and change the rules to fit your group and include activities that would be fun to do in your community. Let the birthday child have some input, but add a couple or three surprises for the day of the birthday party. Here's a sample:

RULES:

1. The "Snickle" team will be with one adult driver (e.g., mom) and the "Fritz" team will be with the other adult driver (e.g., dad).

2. Each team will be given a Polaroid camera. The entire team is responsible for the camera.

3. The adult driver takes a picture of team member performing each activity (to provide proof they really did it!)

4. All team members must be in each picture.

5. Activities do not have to be done in the order listed.

6. Team members, not the driver, will determine which activity to do and when.

7. The winning team will be determined by the number of activities completed and who is back first.

8. Drivers must not break any laws such as speeding or running red lights.

9. All team members must wear hats at all times.

10. All team members must have FUN!

ACTIVITIES:

❑   Visit a local park and take a picture of all the team members on a slide.

❑   Hug a stranger who is eating pizza.

❑   Find a police officer and have your picture taken with him or her.

❑   Help a stranger carry groceries to his or her car.

❑   Stand in the bathtub of a neighbor's house (it cannot be the tub of anyone attending the party).

❑   Wash all the windows of a stranger's car at a gas station

❑   Take a picture of all team members throwing pennies into a fountain.

❑   Take a picture of the team polishing the headlights of a fire truck. A firefighter must be included in the photo.

❑   _____

❑   _____

The Day Before the Party

❏ Make the cake (if you didn't order one)

❏ Scoop ice cream into baking cups placed in a muffin tin. Put in freezer.

The Day of the Party

❏ Decorate the party area (optional).

❏ Pick up the cake (if you ordered one).

❏ Set up the Crazy Hat and Face Painting areas. Spread plastic tablecloths on the ground and set out the art materials shown on the checklists above (face paints, glue, newspaper, etc.) in cardboard trays.

❏ Decide where you'll hold the Get-Together Time and Present Opening. Clear an area large enough to spread out a blanket or sheet.

❏ Set the table for refreshments or decide where you'll put a tablecloth on the ground.

Let's Party!

When the guests arrive, direct them to the Crazy Hat and Face Painting areas. It's a must-do! All guests must wear a kooky and crazy hat of their own creation before the Citywide Scavenger Hunt can begin!

Make 'n Create

Crazy Hats

Here's how to do it. If you'd rather *see* how than *read* how, turn the page!

1. Lay three whole sheets of newspaper over each guest's head.

2. Place the sheets so they are criss-crossed (not straight).

3. Mold the paper around the guest's head -- have the guest cover her ears with her hands. Ask, "Can you breathe? Are you scared? Can you see?"

4. Wrap packaging tape around the head at ear level -- have guests remove their hands when you come to the ears -- make the hats fairly snug.

5. Shape the brims of the hat by rolling the ends of the paper -- be careful not to poke the eyes -- towards the center.

6. Fasten the rolled paper down with more tape. Newspaper has a memory and is used to being flat, so the tape is necessary to keep the shape of your brim.

7. Brims can be left big and wide or rolled up tight. You can make a pirate hat or a cowboy hat. Let the guests decide.

8. Paint and decorate the hat with colored glue and art materials. How crazy and kooky can you make your hat?

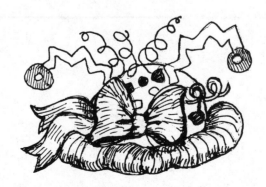

See How It's Done!

Face Painting & Tattoos

Let guests loose with the face paints and encourage kid-to-kid Face Painting. Tell them to be sure to stay at least an inch away from a person's eyes with all face paints and tattoos.

Cheek art is very popular -- you might want to provide some samples of ideas on a piece of paper for those who get stuck -- hearts, rainbows, clouds, birds, trees, flowers, butterflies, unicorns, dragons, flying bats, skull & bones, dogs, teddy bears, stars, moons, lightning bolts, balloons, etc.

If guests don't want to have their cheeks painted, maybe they'd like a painting on their hands or arms.

Tattoos can go just about anywhere. Kids of all ages love them as they instantly produce a realistic drawing with a little water and patience. No adults required after just one demonstration. Guests can tattoo themselves or ask a friend for help with hard to reach places.

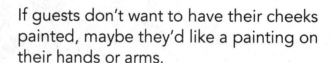

Kid-to-Kid

Encourage kid-to-kid face painting. You'll be amazed at the creative designs kids come up with. Watch out, or you might get painted too! (And why not? It's fun to let the silly sides of ourselves come out once in awhile.)

Hysterical Documentation

Using the Polaroid camera, take a candid photo of each guest complete with crazy hat and painted face.

Get-Together Time

Spread out a blanket or sheet and gather guests in a circle sitting around the edge.

The Name Game

This game is based on a 1965 song by Shirley Ellis titled *"The Name Game."* It has rhythm. It keeps time. It has bananas in its rhyme. So, as the banana is tossed from guest to guest, begin the verse by saying the guest's name twice, then rhyming it with the song. Here are some examples:

**Sharron ,Sharron
Bo Barron
Banana Fana Fo Farron
Fi Fie Mo Marron
Sharron!**

Here are a couple more:

**Jamie, Jamie
Bo Bamie
Banana Fana Fo Famie
Fi Fie Mo Mamie
Jamie!**

**Greg, Greg
Bo Beg
Banana Fana Fo Feg
Fi Fie Mo Meg
Greg!**

It shouldn't be too hard to get the hang of this. Have fun as every guest takes a turn holding the banana and hearing the song with his or her name and its silly rhyming version!

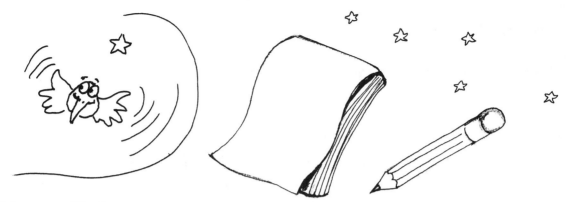

Memory Challenge

1. Place an assortment of ordinary items on a tray/cookie sheet.

2. Seat the guests in a circle with the tray in the middle.

3. Point to each item and have the guests name it.

4. Now cover the tray with a cloth.

5. Give each guest a pencil and a small notebook.

6. Have the guests write down the names of as many items as they can remember.

7. Uncover the tray and let the guests see how many items they remembered.

8. Challenge the guests further by adding new items and moving the items around on the tray.

9. Repeat the game as before.

10. Guests may keep the pencils and notebooks as party favors.

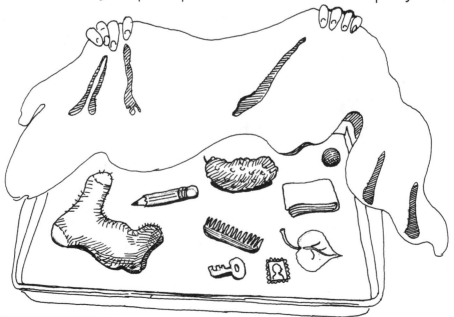

Snicklefritz Partners Switch

You'll need an empty space indoors or outdoors for this game.

1. Guests find partners and stand back to back.

2. An adult will give commands. The partners must react quickly. For example, when the adult says: "Side to Side," the partners touch sides.

3. When the adult says "Snicklefritz Partners Switch," everyone changes partners. Guests must choose a new partner each time.

4. Issue commands (interspersed with "Snicklefritz Partners Switch) in random order. Here are a few to try:

    - Hands to Hands
    - Ear to Ear
    - Ankle to Ankle
    - Elbow to Elbow
    - Knee to Knee
    - Cheek to Cheek
    - Toes to Toes
    - Head to Head

5. After a few commands (depending on the size of your group), end the game and have one of the partners squat down and the other remain standing.

The kids squatting down are the "Snickle" team; the kids standing up are the "Fritz" team. Send teams to opposite sides of the room and tell them they're now ready for the Citywide Scavenger Hunt.

Games & Activities

Citywide Scavenger Hunt

Pass out the Rules and Activities sheets.

Before going out the door:

- ❏ team drivers synchronize their watches,
- ❏ guests put on their Crazy Hats,
- ❏ pass out "thank you" sheets to each team (to give to people who help them complete activities),
- ❏ make sure each team has a Polaroid camera and film.

Now, Ready, Set, Scavenge!

When the teams return from the hunt, there will be lots of talking, picture sharing and funny stories to tell about what happened! Award the rubber chickens to the team members who returned first and similar gag gifts to members of the other team.

Let's Eat!

Follow the basic instructions in the *"High Drama~Serving the Cake"* section in the LET'S PARTY! chapter.

Open Presents

Candid Camera

1. Have guests retrieve the presents they brought and sit in a circle as they did earlier at Get-Together Time.

2. Instruct the guests to put their presents behind their backs.

3. Put the candid photos taken after the guests finished their face painting inside a crazy hat (the birthday child might want to donate his or her hat for the occasion).

4. Seat the birthday child in the middle of the circle with the hat full of photos.

5. The birthday child closes his or her eyes and pulls photo out of the hat.

6. The person whose photo was picked gives the birthday child a present.

7. In turn, the birthday child gives that person the candid photo to keep.

8. After the birthday child and guest exchange "Thank you" and "You're welcome," the birthday child picks another photo from the hat.

9. The game continues until all the guests have given their gifts to the birthday child.

The Party's Over!

Remind guests to take home their crazy hats and candid photos. Don't forget the gag gifts from the scavenger hunt. Perhaps give each guest one or two more gag gifts -- they're favorites. Send home the pencils and small notebooks from the Memory Challenge game.

As guests leave, the birthday child thanks each one individually for making this party the best one *ever*!

ROCK 'N ROLL GLITTER PARTY

This MAKEUP & DANCE PARTY will have all the guests dreaming of Hollywood and leaving with stars in their eyes. It's the perfect *all girl* party (of course, you could adapt the games and activities for any guest list) and it's easy to find mom and teenager assistants! When they're all gussied up, take advantage of the photo opportunity. Include the photo when you send the thank you note. A photo captures the moment. Moms don't often get to see their daughters wearing makeup and coifed hair!

Rock 'n Roll Glitter Party Snapshot

AGES:	**8 TO 12**
TOTAL TIME:	**2 HOURS**

30 minutes
Make 'n Create
Party Bags
Jewelry
Beauty Salon

15 to 20 minutes
Get-Together Time
Toss Your Cookies
Makeup Mix-up
Hand Jive

20 to 30 minutes
Games & Activities
Hula Hoop Play
Driving with Hoops
Musical Hoops
Streamer Ribbon Dancing
Limbo
Partner Twist

15 to 20 minutes
Let's Eat!
Cake
Ice Cream
Blue Hawaii's

15 to 20 minutes
Open Presents
Spin the Bottle

Get Ready!

Invitations

☐ Make up your own or copy and send out the Beauty Salon
Appointment Slip shown below. Let your daughter fill in the blanks
with her name, date, time, address and phone number.

Checklists

Party Bags

- ❑ white paper lunch bags
- ❑ colored markers
- ❑ stickers (some with alphabet letters)
- ❑ rubber stamps, stamp pads

> **THIS ROCK 'N ROLL PARTY ANIMAL SAYS:** *Plan party shopping so you and your daughter can do it together.*

Supplies & Decorations

- ❑ paper products (tablecloth, plates, napkins)
- ❑ clear plastic cups for drinks (Blue Hawaii's are pretty to look at!)
- ❑ utensils (plastic fork, spoon)
- ❑ balloons/streamers

Beauty Salon

Buy inexpensive makeup from drugstores or discount stores; check your supplies for old makeup and ask your friends for donations. (Use only new makeup for eyes to avoid contamination.) Collect 2-3 of each of the following (different colors are fun to try!):

- ❑ foundation
- ❑ blusher
- ❑ eye shadow
- ❑ lipstick
- ❑ mascara
- ❑ eye pencils or liners
- ❑ mirrors (several)
- ❑ nail polish
- ❑ nail polish remover
- ❑ nail decals

- ❑ cotton squares or balls
- ❑ Q-Tips
- ❑ Kleenex
- ❑ paper towels
- ❑ hairbrushes and combs
- ❑ roll-on glitter (you'll find it with costume makeup at party supply stores)
- ❑ glitter hair gel/hair sprays
- ❑ fluorescent hair color sprays

Jewelry

Here's what you'll need for necklaces, bracelets and earrings:

- ❏ stick-on earrings
- ❏ plastic or wooden beads (assorted shapes and colors)
- ❏ string, lanyard or elastic cord for stringing necklaces or bracelets

Get-Together Time

- ❑ small box of animal shaped cookies
- ❑ 8-10 makeup or glamour items, e.g., lipstick, compact/mirror, comb, brush, nail polish, hair spray, cotton ball, costume jewelry earring, bracelet, necklace
- ❑ large scarf
- ❑ music: *"Born to Hand Jive"* by Sha Na Na from the original movie soundtrack for Grease
- ❑ CD or tape player

Games & Activities

- ❑ one Hula Hoop per guest
- ❑ one metallic waving streamer for each guest (order from one of the catalogs or make your own with mylar ribbon and sticks)

- ❑ music: *"The Limbo"* and *"The Twist"* from the tapes or CD's Dancin' Magic by Joanie Bartels or Greatest Hits by Chubby Checker.
- ❑ limbo stick (a broom handle will work)

Refreshments

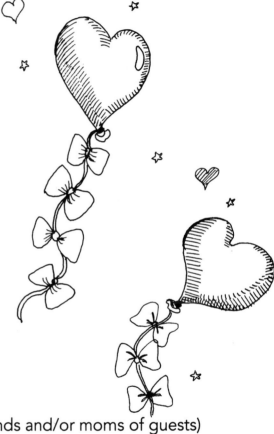

- ❑ make or purchase a cake
- ❑ ice cream? or how about sorbet or sherbet for this party!
- ❑ muffin or cupcake paper liners and muffin tin
- ❑ Blue Hawaii ingredients
    - ✱ liter bottles of 7-Up
    - ✱ maraschino cherries
    - ✱ blue food coloring
    - ✱ ice cube trays
- ❑ punch bowl (optional)

Present Opening

- ❑ an empty, clean Coca-Cola bottle

Don't Forget

- ❑ candles and matches
- ❑ camera
- ❑ video camera
- ❑ tape or CD player
- ❑ film
- ❑ 3 helpers (spouse, relative, teenagers, friends and/or moms of guests)
- ❑ back-up batteries for CD or tape player and cameras

Get Set!

The Day Before the Party

- ❏ Make the cake (if that was your daughter's choice).

- ❏ Drop a maraschino cherry into each section of an ice cube tray, fill the tray with water and freeze.

- ❏ Scoop ice cream, sorbet or sherbet into cupcake paper liners placed in a muffin tin. Put into freezer.

- ❏ Cut elastic cord, string or lanyard into 36" lengths for necklaces and 12" lengths for bracelets (knot one end of each piece).

The Day of the Party

- ❏ Decorate the party area.

- ❏ Pick-up the cake if you ordered one.

- ❏ Spread out blankets or sheets and materials for each of the Make 'n Create areas:
  - * Party Bags
  - * Beauty Salon
  - * Jewelry Making

- ❏ Decide where you'll hold the Get-Together Time and Present Opening. You'll need to clear enough space to spread a blanket or sheet to sit around.

- ❏ Prepare the yard for Games & Activities. (Clear enough open space to move in freely. Check to make sure the yard's free of mementos from any pets!)

- ❏ Set the table for refreshments or plan where you'll put a tablecloth on the ground.

Let's Party

Make 'n Create

Station "beauty assistants" at the Make 'n Create areas. When guests arrive, send them to the Party Bag making area. When they're done at one area, guests proceed to another until they've completed all three.

Party Bags

- ❏ Give each guest a flat white lunch bag and ask them to decorate only the front of the bag.

- ❏ Guests write their names on the bags or make their names out of alphabet stickers.

- ❏ Guests decorate their party bags.

Jewelry Making

- ☺ Give each guest a length of elastic cord for making a necklace or bracelet (they can do both if time allows).

- ☺ Guests string cord with beads. Girls in this age bracket usually are very creative and imaginative in developing patterns or designs.

- ☺ When guests finish their jewelry piece, tie the ends together in a knot and cut off any excess cord. Guests can wear their jewelry now or put it in their party bags.

- ☺ Allow guests to choose a pair of stick-on earrings to wear on their ears or as "body jewels" (on face, etc.)

Beauty Salon

❤ Show guests the available makeup items and cosmetics.

❤ Encourage guests to help each other -- from applying makeup to painting each other's nails. Helper's main focus is to gel hair or spray with fluorescent colors (be careful of eyes, headbands, bows and clips).

❤ Take each beauty's picture when she's done!

Get-Together Time

Spread out a blanket or sheet and gather the guests into a circle sitting around the perimeter of the blanket. Tell them they're going to play a name game to identify and recognize all who came to your child's house in honor of her birthday.

Toss Your Cookies

Encourage all the guests to join in and chant as they toss the box of animal shaped cookies from person to person. Fill in the blank with the name of the child who catches the cookies.

(everyone chants...)
Who stole the cookies from the cookie jar?

(toss cookies to a guest)
_____ stole the cookies from the cookie jar.

(child who is holding cookies says...)
Who me?

(guests all point their fingers at her and chant...)
Yes, you.

(child holding cookies says...)
Couldn't be!

(guests say...)
Then who?

(child holding cookies tosses box to a child who hasn't had a turn
and everyone chants...)
Who stole the cookies from the cookie jar?

(all say...)
_____ stole the cookies form the cookie jar.

Continue the game until each guest has taken a turn tossing the cookies.

Makeup Mix-up

Guests don't need a photographic mind, but it sure helps when you play this game. You'll find that the youngsters do better than the oldsters.

Still sitting in a circle, show the guests the makeup and glamour items one at a time.

1. Have at least as many items as the Birthday Girl is old.

2. Name each item, then cover all the items with a scarf.

3. Say "abracadabra" (or any "magic words" the birthday star conjures up) and wave one hand over the scarf.

4. Remove one item, concealing it with the scarf, as you lift up the scarf (Don't let the guests see what you've removed.)

5. Ask who can guess which item is missing.

6. Continue the game, waving two hands over the scarf while saying the magic words. Remove two or more items when you lift the scarf.

7. Ask guests who haven't already answered to name the missing items.

8. On the final wave over the scarf, shake both hands (for really strong magic!) while saying the magic words and remove all the items when you lift up the scarf.

9. Ask the guests who have not had a turn to name the missing items.

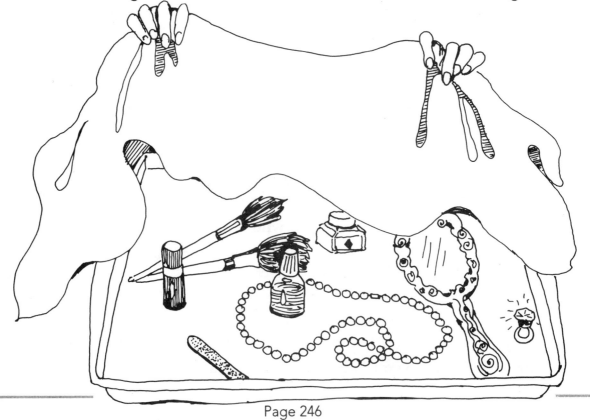

Hand Jive

Before doing this to music, teach the guests the following hand motions:

1. Slap thighs twice.

2. Clap hands twice.

3. With palms down, cross and uncross hands (right hand on top) in front of you, twice.

4. With palms down cross and uncross hands (left hand on top) in front of you twice.

5. Pound fists (right fist on top) twice.

6. Pound fists (left fist on top) twice.

7. Hitchhike (right hand) twice.

8. Hitchhike (left hand) twice.

9. Repeat the entire sequence.

When guests seem to have the hang of it, turn on the music, catch the rhythm and hand jive till you can't do it one more time!!

Games & Activities

Intersperse these games before and after refreshments or present opening. But be sure to do at least one, if not two, of the activities before sitting down to eat.

You or one of your helpers can easily lead these games by following the step-by-step directions. Your birthday child will feel like "Queen For The Day" if the two of you rehearse and practice these games before the actual day of her party. Have a CD or tape player ready and a song picked out from the music you collected.

Start out by giving each child a Hula Hoop and some time to fool around and experiment with it before you start the games. Tell the guests they get to take the Hula Hoops home as party favors. *Hooray*!

Driving with Hoops

1. Instruct the girls to put their Hula Hoops on the ground and stand inside them.

2. Tell them the Hula Hoops are their steering wheels. When the music starts, they lift the hoop up to waist level and use both hands to turn it right and left as if driving while they walk around in the space available in the yard.

3. When the music stops, they drop their hoops to the ground as if they've reached a stop sign or stoplight.

4. When the music starts again, they pick up their hoops and continue to drive.

5. Fun ensues when you start and stop the music for short intervals or keep it on for long stretches. Add some dialogue to the game by mentioning that they may be caught speeding if going too fast.

6. The game lasts the length of one song.

Musical Hoops

Each child puts her hoop down on the ground and stands beside it.

1. Start the music and instruct the children to walk around the hoops, making sure not to touch any of them while the music is playing.

2. When the music stops, each child steps into the nearest hoop. It's fine if more than one child ends up in one hoop. In fact, encourage it!

3. Start the music again and remove a hoop or two. When the music stops, the children step into the nearest hoop.

4. The game continues, with you gathering up more hoops and the children scrambling to all fit into the remaining hoops.

5. Musical Hoops ends with one or two hoops on the floor and all of the girls working together to make sure everyone finds a place inside a hoop. It's crowded but lots of fun!

For variety ask the birthday child which way the guests should travel around the hoops. Besides walking or running perhaps they could skip, tiptoe, or even walk backwards. Suggest they travel a different way each time the music starts again.

Streamer Ribbon Dancing

The streamer is not only a piece of equipment used to play the game but also doubles as a party favor!

1. Give each guest a streamer ribbon.

2. Select music (fast and slow) from the music you collected for the party.

3. With streamer ribbons in hand, children start dancing when the music starts. When the music stops, they freeze.

4. Children resume dancing when the music starts again.

5. Stop and re-start the music. Each time, provide the guests with a new challenge, e.g., ask them to dance in their...

    * *high space* (streamer ribbons above their heads, dancing on their tiptoes).

    * *low space* (squatting down, keeping streamer ribbons low to the ground).

    * *middle space* (streamer ribbons at waist height).

6. Try to trick the dancers by starting and stopping the music quickly. They love the element of surprise!

Vary the tempo of the game by playing a slow selection and suggesting the children twirl, leap and float to the music.

Limbo

This is a favorite classic and one that needs little introduction except its name.

☆ Two helpers hold the ends of the limbo stick.

☆ Guests line-up behind the birthday child on one side of stick.

☆ Start the music. Each child takes a turn dancing under the limbo stick.

☆ When the birthday child comes to the front of the line, lower the limbo stick.

☆ Continue to lower the stick each time the birthday child comes around.

☆ Allow the guests to go under the stick any creative way they desire as long as they don't hurt themselves or others.

You may have to stop the game for a moment to rewind the tape or restart the CD as the dance usually lasts longer than the song. Limbo ends when there's no more space for children to dance under.

Partner Twist

Stand in place and twist your feet and arms from side-to-side. You're doing the Twist!

- ✸ Guests find partners.
- ✸ When the music starts, guests dance the twist with their partner.
- ✸ When the music stops, the guests find new partners.
- ✸ When the music starts again, the guests "twist the night away" with their new partners.
- ✸ Game continues with children finding a partner they haven't "twisted" with every time the music stops.

Partner Twist ends when everyone has danced with everyone else or when the song ends.

Let's Eat!

Refer to the *"High Drama~Serving the Cake"* section in the LET'S PARTY! chapter for the basics, but add the Blue Hawaii special touch for this special party. Ask a helper to prepare Blue Hawaii's while the guests finish their last game.

It's as easy as 1-2-3:

1.   Pour 7-Up into the punch bowl.
2.   Tint the 7-Up with a small amount of blue food coloring.
3.   Float maraschino cherry ice cubes in the blue 7-Up.

Guests serve themselves with punch ladle. One ice cube per guest!

Open Presents

For more specifics about present opening refer to the *"Opening Presents~The Center of Attention!"* section in the LET'S PARTY! chapter.

Spin the Bottle

- ⇨ Have the guests sit in a circle, placing their presents behind their backs.

- ⇨ Seat the birthday child in the middle of the circle with the empty Coca-Cola bottle.

- ⇨ The birthday child spins the bottle.

- ⇨ The guest the bottle points to gives their present to the birthday child.

- ⇨ Continue the game until all the presents have been given to the birthday child.

The Party's Over!

Guests gather party bags which hold their necklaces, bracelets and streamer ribbons. Don't forget to send a Hula Hoop home with each guest, too.

As guests leave, the birthday girl thanks each one individually for joining her in:

Games & Activities

Get-Together Time

Make 'n Create

The Party's Over!